Being, Becoming and Behavior

THE PSYCHOLOGICAL SCIENCES

Being, Becoming and Behavior

THE PSYCHOLOGICAL SCIENCES

Edited with Introductions by

FLOYD W. MATSON

GEORGE BRAZILLER
NEW YORK

For information, address the publisher:
George Braziller, Inc.
One Park Avenue
New York, N.Y. 10016

Library of Congress Catalog Card Number: 67–24208
First Printing
Printed in the United States of America

TO

Ashley and Marjorie Montagu

ACKNOWLEDGMENTS

The editor and publisher wish to thank the following for permission to reprint the material included in this anthology:

AMERICAN PSYCHOLOGICAL ASSOCIATION—for "The Reflex Arc Concept in Psychology," by John Dewey, from *Psychological Review*, 1896; "Mind, Mechanism and Adaptive Behavior," by Clark L. Hull, from *Psychological Review*, 1937; and "Perception and Gestalt Psychology," from Kurt Koffka, "Perception: An Introduction to the Gestalt-Theorie," in *Psychological Bulletin*, 1922.

GREENBERG PUBLISHER, INC.—for "The Style of Life," from *The Science of Living* by Alfred Adler. Copyright © 1929 by Greenberg Publisher, Inc., © 1957 by Kurt Adler.

GRUNE AND STRATTON, INC.—for "Existential Analysis and Psychotherapy," by Ludwig Binswanger, from *Progress in Psychotherapy: 1956*, edited by F. Fromm-Reichmann and J. L. Moreno.

HOLT, RINEHART AND WINSTON, INC.—for "The Human Situation," from *The Sane Society* by Erich Fromm. Copyright © 1955 by Erich Fromm.

HOUGHTON MIFFLIN COMPANY—for "Elements of Psychophysics," from *Elemente der Psychophysik* by Gustav Fechner, Leipzig, 1860, translated by Herbert Sidney Langfeld. Taken from Benjamin Rand, ed., *The Classical Psychologists*, Houghton Mifflin, 1912.

LITTLE, BROWN & COMPANY—for selection from *The Undiscovered Self* by Carl Gustav Jung. Copyright © 1958 by Carl G. Jung.

THE MACMILLAN COMPANY—for "The Problem of Control," from *Science and Human Behavior* by B. F. Skinner. Copyright © 1953 by The Macmillan Company.

W. W. NORTON & COMPANY, INC.—for selections from *The Interpersonal Theory of Psychiatry* by Harry Stack Sullivan, M.D.; copyright 1953 by The William Alanson White Psychiatric Foundation. And "What Is Behaviorism?" from *Behaviorism* by John B. Watson; copyright 1924, 1925 by John B. Watson; copyright 1930, revised edition, by W. W. Norton & Company, Inc. and renewed © 1958 by John B. Watson.

W. W. NORTON & COMPANY, INC. AND THE HOGARTH PRESS, LTD.—for "The Theory of Instincts," from *An Outline of Psychoanalysis* by Sigmund Freud; authorized translation by James Strachey. Copyright 1949 by W. W. Norton & Company, Inc.

OPEN COURT PUBLISHING COMPANY, LA SALLE, ILLINOIS—for "Man—A Machine," from *L'Homme machine*, by Julien de la Mettrie, 1748, translated by G. C. Bussey and M. W. Calkins as *Man—A Machine*.

PHILOSOPHICAL LIBRARY—for "Early Treatment of the Mentally Ill," from *One Hundred Years of Psychiatry* by Emil Kraepelin; "On Conditioned Reflexes," from *Experimental Psychology* by Ivan Pavlov as it appears in *Essays in Psychology and Psychiatry* by Ivan Pavlov.

RANDOM HOUSE, INC.—for "Two Divergent Trends," by Carl R. Rogers from *Existential Psychology*, edited by Rollo May, Random House, 1961.

HENRY REGNERY COMPANY—for "The Will to Power," from *Beyond Good and Evil* by Friedrich Nietzsche, translated by Marianne Cowan, Henry Regnery Company, Chicago, 1955.

ROUTLEDGE AND KEGAN PAUL, LTD.—for selection from *Man in the Modern Age* by Karl Jaspers.

H. D. SPOERL—for a selection from *General Psychology from the Personalistic Standpoint* by William Stern, translated by H. D. Spoerl. Copyright H. D. Spoerl.

D. VAN NOSTRAND COMPANY, INC.—for "Toward a Psychology of Health," from *Toward a Psychology of Being* by Abraham H. Maslow.

YALE UNIVERSITY PRESS—for "Becoming: The Dilemma of Uniqueness," from *Becoming: Basic Considerations for a Psychology of Personality* by Gordon W. Allport; for "A Clue to the Nature of Man: The Symbol," *An Essay on Man* by Ernst Cassirer, © 1944 by Yale University Press; *The Courage to Be* by Paul Tillich, Yale paperbound edition 1959, copyright 1952 by Yale University Press.

The editor and publisher have made every effort to determine and credit the holders of copyrights of the selections in this book. Any errors or omissions will be rectified in future editions.

Being, Becoming and Behavior

THE PSYCHOLOGICAL SCIENCES

Contents

Introduction

BEING, BECOMING AND BEHAVIOR

Psychology is the systematic effort to understand the inner experience and outer behavior of human beings. Like other capsule definitions of complex matters, this one is doubtless both overinflated and underinclusive. For the term "psychology" refers to an elastic field of study which has varied widely, not to say wildly, in its scope and method from time to time and from place to place. Nor, even in a given time such as our own, is there much consensus regarding the boundaries and promontories of the field. "Except for a common loyalty to their profession," according to Gordon W. Allport, "psychologists often seem to agree on little else. ... Some definitions of psychology put the stress on *experience*, some on *behavior*, others on *psychophysical relations*, some on *conscious mental processes*, some on the *unconscious*, others on *human nature*, a few on 'the *totality of man's psychic existence.*' "[1]

The extent of the disagreement among psychologists in the delineation of their subject matter may be illustrated by reference to one of the oldest conceptual approaches in the field, and to one of the most recent. The first great psychol-

1

ogist in the Western tradition, Socrates of Athens, defined his vocation as the examination and improvement of the soul *(psyche)*. Indeed, it was Socrates who "discovered" the soul—and who, not content to describe and classify his find, sought persistently and at the risk of life itself to help others in the proper use of this uniquely human possession.[2] (With his equal interest in examination and exhortation, the twin methods of dialectic, Socrates might well be characterized as both a research psychologist and a practicing psychotherapist.)

At the other extreme of the scale of possibilities, the founder of the behaviorist school of psychology, early in the twentieth century, publicly banished the *psyche* from his realm. The modern psychologist, said John B. Watson, had to begin by "sweeping aside all medieval conceptions. He dropped from his scientific vocabulary all subjective terms such as sensation, perception, image, desire, purpose, and even thinking and emotion as they were subjectively defined."[3] In short, as Gardner Murphy has put it, behaviorism was "a psychology without a soul." Two thousand years after Socrates, his great discovery—that of the inner life of man— was discarded as irrelevant to psychology.

In a sense, this book is the history of what happened in psychology during the two millennia between the metaphorical birth and death of the soul. But let it be said at once that, in the nature of things (specifically of books and editors), such a history can be neither comprehensive nor wholly objective. Whatever may be the capacity of men to mold their future, it is certain that they continuously remake their past. Nowhere is the faculty known to psychologists as selective perception more at work than in our dogged search through the archives for some sign of ourselves—or, it may be, some sign *for* ourselves.

This book is no exception. It undertakes to document and illustrate certain themes and issues in the literature of psychology which are among the most recurrent, representative, and relevant. More than that, it seeks to call attention to certain pioneers and pathfinders of the remote or recent past, whose numbers include some of the wisest and best minds our civilization has produced. Their reflections are surely worth preserving and prizing, whatever the current status of their reputations as theorists. Pinel, for example—whose personal nobility most closely approaches that of Socrates—was not only a great psychiatrist but a great human being. In his courageous act of commitment to the ideals of 1789—defying ages of vicious superstition and prejudice by personally striking the chains from the wretched inmates of the madhouse at Bicêtre, liberating them at a stroke from bedlam to humanity, and with the same stroke inaugurating a revolution in psychiatry—this shy and modest healer of the Enlightenment fulfilled, in the most literal sense, the condition laid down in our own time by Ludwig Binswanger for the truly existential psychotherapist: that he "dare to risk committing his own existence in the struggle for the freedom of his partner's."

The essays here collected may (it is therefore hoped) be read for pleasure, as the personal testimony of men of genius, as well as studied with profit as scientific documents. But even the dichotomy of the "two cultures" (the sciences and the humanities), which that option suggests, is no longer quite tenable. It is a tribute to the refreshingly unconventional conjectures of numbers of eminent scientists in recent years that we need no longer regard it as forbidden to have our scientific cake and eat it with enjoyment too. We know now that the works of science at their best—like those of poetry at their best—are acts of creation, conceived in wonderment and pursued with passion; that they are the acts not of gods or machines, but of doubting, fretful, "sleepwalking" human persons. Whatever else it may be, as Jacques Barzun has had the courage to declare, science is a "glorious entertainment."[4]

This is not to say that there are no distinctions between the scientific experience and, for example, the religious experience or the sexual experience. But we have been told the whole truth about those distinctions, and nothing but those distinctions, for a long time now. It may be that the time has come to relax somewhat the vigilant watch o'er the ramparts of the scientific establishment against the intrusion and infection of all that is valued, all that is felt, all that is incorrigibly human. It may be time to spare some amount of serious attention to the exploration of common frontiers and common denominators—to the "common sense of science." To emphasize the *humanity* of science is warranted in any context; but it is indispensable in connection with the science of humanity. It is indispensable, to be blunt about it, in order to avert what a distinguished mathematical physicist (Norbert Wiener) has called "the inhuman use of human beings"—in the name of science. One recalls the remark of Lewis Mumford that the dramatic boast of a scientific true believer—"I shall follow the Truth wherever it may lead, though the Heavens fall!"—could never have been uttered at all after that summer day in 1945 when stars fell on Hiroshima and made an end of innocence.[5]

The study of psychology is both a peculiar variety of scientific experience and a special kind of human experience: it is man reflecting on his own nature. The psychologist is a scientist who has exchanged his microscope and telescope for a full-length mirror; his is the one science where the observer is also the observed. To be sure, this is not the customary view of the matter. Much of the history of scientific psychology is the record of successive ingenious attempts to deny the force of this realization and to escape its theoretical consequences. Two mechanisms of escape in particular have been commonly employed: the definition of the observer as *more* than human (i.e., nonattached, bias-free and value-neutral), and the definition of the observed as *less* than human (i.e., as an object in nature). These twin efforts at transcendence and reduction continue unabated in the laboratories and lecture halls of the present day; but the voices of dissent are also heard in the land, a rising chorus echoing, in a variety of specialist vocabularies, the insight well expressed by the late Percy W. Bridgman: that in science as elsewhere in life we cannot get away from ourselves—there is no escaping the human reference point.[6]

It might be supposed that psychology shares with the humanities (as distinct from the social sciences) an additional attribute: namely, that its proper study is not mankind in general but man in particular; its concern is with the individual rather than with the group, the culture, or the society. There are, however, two difficulties with this supposition. One has to do with the categorical distinction between the individual (psychology) and the social (sociology); for it can be argued, on the one hand, that individual psychology is at bottom the study of interpersonal or social relations, and on the other hand that all of social science is merely an extrapolation from the psychology of the individual.[7] In either case the distinction between the individual and the social disappears.

The second difficulty with the assumption that psychology is engaged with the individual human being is that so many psychologists appear to disregard the person, both in his wholeness and his uniqueness, in favor of one or another of

his constituent parts, elements, traits, drives, instincts, biological processes, or mechanical analogies.[8] By the 1960's, the
suspicion that American psychology in its dominant schools
and concepts had lost all contact with the human person was
sufficiently widespread to bring about the formation of a
vigorous independent movement in the field centered upon
the American Association for Humanistic Psychology—while
at the same time stimulating the production of a noteworthy
number of volumes conveying the same portent and protest.[9]

To some extent the contemporary collision between the
"humanists" and the "scientists" (or mechanists) of psychology represents only the latest rematch of a pair of age-old
and tireless antagonists. In the most ancient quarrel of all—
the body-mind problem—the issue was drawn along similar
lines. Materialism (body) has been a scientific dogma even
longer than it has been a political ideology and a social
gospel, while its venerable adversary Idealism (mind) has
had a host of incarnations: vitalism, holism, romanticism,
personalism, phenomenology, and existentialism, to name a
few. The great and vexed issues in the history of psychology,
if they have not always reflected the same confrontation of
forces, have consistently exposed a difference of viewpoint
and outlook which cuts so deep as to seem rooted in character
and temperament. It was this intuition of a fundamental
division of assumptive frames of reference that William
James had in mind when he broached his famous dichotomy
between the Tough-minded and Tender-minded styles.[10]
But James, whatever his intention, was not playing quite
fair; his way of posing the alternatives begs the question and
prejudices the issue—at least for most of us moderns. For, as
the loaded labels "tough" and "tender" suggest, one style
appropriates the manly virtues of realism, conviction, and—
most dear of all—rigor, while the other conjures up the girlish

frailties of sentimentality, ambivalence, and soft confusion. Pollyanna is no match for Prometheus.

Looked at another way, however, with only a slight shift of standpoint and perspective, the issue becomes a very different one. Thus the classic problem of free will versus determinism changes the alignment radically; here Prometheus (an existentialist hero if there ever was one) has abandoned the ranks of rigor and "realism" and gone over to the other side. All the challenge and chance, change and choice are on the side of voluntarism; the alternative of determinism may become the reluctant recourse of hardliners and bitter-enders, but there is no glamour or gaiety in it. Psychologists indeed have been more deeply and persistently divided over this particular issue than any other—ever since Socrates on his deathbed sought to refute the materialist argument of his young friends that his behavior was determined by involuntary physical causes:

> For, by the Dog! these bones and sinews, I think, would have been somewhere near Megara and Boeotia long ago, carried there by an opinion of what is best, if I had not believed it better and more just to submit to any sentence which my city gives than to take to my heels and run. But to call such things causes is strange indeed. If one should say that unless I had such things, bones and sinews and all the rest I have, I should not have been able to do what I thought best, that would be true; but to say that these, and not my choice of the best, are the causes of my doing what I do . . . would be a very far-fetched and slovenly way of speaking.[11]

Not all of the theoretical controversies which have racked and enlivened the history of psychology are, to be sure, translatable into the dramatic dilemmas suggested by the philosophical categories of freedom and determinism. But it is remarkable how many such disputes—nature-nurture, activity-structure, heredity-environment, reductionism-holism,

faculty-association, introspectionism-behaviorism—have re-
volved around these metaphysical poles. Nor should that fact
surprise us. The foundations of psychology are deeply
grounded in philosophy, having emerged from the parent
discipline into the status of an independent study only within
the past century. Moreover, if it may be said that a hundred
years ago the psychologists were all philosophers, it is almost
as true to say that today the philosophers are all psychologists.
So are we all, of course: Our post-Freudian, postwar, post-
atomic generation is very much (as the truism has it) the
Age of Psychology— the era of Psychological Man.[12] Philosophers too, for all their pretensions to Olympus, are creatures
of their time and intellectual climate; and their current
reworking of the traditional themes of moral discourse and
political theory reveals their debt to the contributions of
modern psychology.[13] But this is only another way of saying
that, at the base and at the spire, psychology and philosophy
are joined.

Apart from its historic connection with philosophy, there
is another reason for the concern that psychologists have
shown for the determinist-voluntarist puzzle. Human behavior can be observed from either of two (and only two)
standpoints: from within and from without. The first approach is that of introspection; the second is that of objective
observation. The first method takes into account the range
of inner experience—purposes, values, reasons, goals; the
second method deliberately limits its field of vision to the
operations of overt behavior. Something of the wide difference between these two perspectives was pointed out a generation ago by the philosopher Warner Fite: "... where the
observer looks for *causes* the agent [actor] expects to find
reasons. What the observer views as a relation of cause and

effect is for the agent a relation of ground and consequence.
For the observer the moving term is a blind force, for the
agent it is a conception of value. In a word, the observer's
view is mechanical, the agent's is logical and teleological."[14]
More recently the distinguished scientist-philosopher, Michael
Polanyi, has underlined this essential distinction in a noteworthy passage:

> *The most important pair of mutually exclusive approaches to
> the same situation is formed by the alternative interpretations of
> human affairs in terms of causes and reasons. You can try to
> represent human actions completely in terms of their natural
> causes. . . . If you carry this out and regard the actions of men,
> including the expression of their convictions, wholly as a set
> of responses to a given set of stimuli, then you obliterate any
> grounds on which the justification of those actions or convictions
> could be given or disputed. You can interpret, for example, this
> essay in terms of the* causes *which have determined my action of
> writing it down or you may ask for my* reasons *for saying what
> I say. But the two approaches—in terms of causes and reasons—
> mutually exclude each other.*[15]

Psychology, it seems, recapitulates cosmology. The images
men hold of the nature of the universe and of their stature
in it provide the referential frames and govern the heuristic
outlines of their images of self. When, as in the Middle Ages,
the world was seen as radiant with purpose and value, so
were the minds and actions of men. Medieval "psychology,"
from Tertullian to Aquinas, was an integral aspect of a
thoroughly teleological system; a system of which every part
was meaningful, significant, valuable. At the heart of the
cosmology—or, rather, at the summit of the great chain of
being—was man: not men in general, nor mankind in the
abstract, but *man in person*. The great contribution of
Christianity to psychology was this concept of the human
person—imperfect but rational, fallen yet endowed with

dignity. The idea of the person conveyed a new recognition of man, not as scientific object but as moral subject; not some*thing* to be treated as a means but some*one* to be cherished, held sacred, as an end in himself. For scholars like Boethius, as Friedrich Heer has reminded us, the greatest beatitude was to be found in the right combination of thought and act—in the cognition of the true and the practice of the good. "Man's intellect must guide him to the discovery of both the good and the true, for if there is anything divine in man then it is the intellect, and it is by the exercise of intellect that truth and justice are discerned and practiced: intellect, truth and right conduct make up the trinity of human beatitude."[16]

Approximately three and a half centuries ago that world view came to an end, not with a bang but a whimper. The Medieval Synthesis of Aquinas and Boethius gave way to the Modern Analysis of Galileo and Newton; the Dantesque vision of Divine Order, of the Harmony of the Spheres, was replaced by the efficient spectacle of the Great Machine— the automated universe. Among the attributes of the old system which went into the discard was the intuition of purpose, the sense of value. "The world that people had thought themselves living in," as E. A. Burtt has put it, "a world rich with colour and sound, redolent with fragrance, filled with gladness, love and creative ideals—was crowded now into minute corners in the brains of scattered organic beings. The really important world outside was a world hard, cold, colourless, silent and dead. . . ."[17]

For a time the Cartesian compromise, the dualism of Descartes, sought to hold the line at that point: The empire of advancing science would be limited to the "world outside," with the inner sanctum of mind (*res cogitans*) kept free. But the pact was soon broken, and the mechanized legions of the new order swept all but unopposed over the frontiers of the mind—abolishing its independence and incorporating it within the universal realm of materialism. By the eighteenth century the victory was total and the surrender seemingly unconditional. Holbach spoke for the new concensus in proclaiming that man was merely an object in nature like any other: "He exists in Nature. He is submitted to her laws. He cannot deliver himself from them." It was only a short step to the next logical inference. "Let us conclude boldly then," said La Mettrie, "that man is a machine, and that there is only one substance, differently modified, in the whole world. What will all the weak reeds of divinity, metaphysics, and nonsense of the schools, avail against this firm and solid oak?"

Suffice it to say that the weak reeds did not avail against the oak. The future of psychology, until well into the twentieth century, was to lie mainly with the scientific movement identified with Newton's celestial mechanics. In their effort to be as rigorous and reliable as the physicists, students of psychology came to be guided by the canons of impersonal objectivity and reductive analysis; that is, they strove on the one hand to maximize the distance of their detachment from the thing observed, and on the other hand to analyze it downward into its working parts and effective causes. The experimental tradition—the main line of evolution in academic psychology during the past century—faithfully pressed this commitment from its origins in organic medicine and physiology, through the great impetus received from animal psychology after Darwin, to its logical culmination in the formidable systems of such behaviorists as Clark L. Hull and B. F. Skinner.

By now there must be scarcely a college student in America who has not been made aware of Skinner's controversial utopian novel, *Walden Two*, published in 1948. In that volume there is acted out a peculiar drama, a fictive projection of a scientific commonwealth which has struck many readers as a nightmare of frightening plausibility, but which was avowedly intended by its author to be a constructive and exhilarating "design for a culture." Skinner, who is the most prominent contemporary spokesman for the school of psychological behaviorism, has spelled out more prosaically elsewhere (notably in *Science and Human Behavior*) his program for a massive application of "behavioral engineering" in the interest of ridding human society once and for all of the onerous burdens of contingency, ambiguity, anxiety, and liberty. In point of fact, none of the moral values and civil traditions which have attended the growth of Western culture find any place in the constitution of Walden Two: not justice, not personal freedom, not even the pursuit of happiness.[18] All that escapes the withering attack of this armed vision is the elemental urge of the tribe and the herd for *survival*. That is to be the goal-value and governing aspiration of the scientific community. All that serves the survival of the group is good; all that resists or opposes it is evil. The new scientific ethic of behaviorist psychology thus turns out to be identical with the oldest ethic of all: that of the struggle for survival, the ethic of the jungle and the swamp.

With this unhappy denouement, the "meta-psychology" of behaviorism would appear to have come full circle—back to its beginning in the authoritarian image of Hobbes' *Leviathan*: the image of a determinate and determining social order in which the individual, shorn of responsibility if not of humanity, plays out a role of microscopic dimensions within a giant body politic in which all events and behaviors proceed with predictable regularity on the basis of calculated stimuli and conditioned responses. There are here no choices to be made, only reactions to be awaited; no spontaneity, only feedback; no Socratic questing or questioning, only a willing suspension of the capacity for wonder. No deviant urges or restless longings mar the placid surface of this remarkable Walden Pond. (How ironic, not to say mischievous, it is for the author-psychologist to appropriate that title, of all titles, to label an imaginary community so contrary to the character and commitment of Thoreau as to seem a monstrous joke. But this narrative is no joke; and the irony is only deepened when it is recognized to be unconscious. The point of the original *Walden* is not only blunted, it is turned in upon itself: for the psychological premise of Thoreau's writing is the very antithesis of Skinner's, and nothing is more certain than that in the manufactured tranquillity and conditioned conformity of Walden Two the resident of Walden *One* would be a stranger and an outcast. "If a man does not keep pace with his companions, perhaps it is because he hears a different drummer. Let him step to the music which he hears, however measured or far away." That is the answer of a free man to the behavioral engineer and the scientific designer of cultures.)

But if the deterministic heirs of Hobbes and La Mettrie have occupied the mainstream of academic psychology in our century, they have not had it all their own way. The most powerful challenge to their dominant position has come, of course, from psychoanalysis and psychotherapy—with their effective combination of the modern science of mind and the ancient art of healing. Where the experimental psychologist has restricted himself to the observation of outer behavior, the "depth" psychologist turns his attention unashamedly to the probing of inner experience. Where the behaviorist disregards the mind except as epiphenomenon or *deus ex machina*, the psychoanalyst regards the mind as having independent reality and potential responsibility. Built into the psychoanalytic approach is a more active and dynamic conception of mind; the dialogue of therapy plainly rests upon the rationalist faith that men may know the truth (about themselves) and that the truth will set them free.

Unfortunately the case is not as simple as that. If the *therapeutic* assumption of nearly all schools of psychoanalysis is constructive and ultimately optimistic, the trend of psychoanalytic *theory* has frequently been in the opposite direction. Few theorists, indeed, have exceeded in pessimism the grim formulations and forebodings of the father of psychoanalysis. For Sigmund Freud all human existence, both individual and collective, was a struggle between aggressive instinctual demands (rooted in the id) and the requirements of culture (incorporated into the superego) —a struggle theoretically without end, if not also without hope. Neither the original nature of men nor the quality of civilization held much constructive possibility: Society was a repressive tyrant demanding obedience, while men—whenever the bonds that held them were "for a moment relaxed"—were merely "savage beasts to whom the thought of sparing their own kind is alien."

Freud's theory of the instincts, based upon a pleasure-principle strikingly reminiscent of the Utilitarian economists of a century before, originally centered upon the sexual drive (libido) as the elemental governing force of human nature. Later he added to this life-force of *Eros* an independent instinct of aggression and destruction, literally a death-force, to which he gave the classical title of *Thanatos*. "This instinct of aggression is the derivative and main representative of the death instinct we have found alongside of Eros, sharing his rule over the earth." But the two rulers are not compatible; each constantly seeks to overthrow the other. "And now, it seems to me, the meaning of the evolution of culture is no longer a riddle to us. It must present to us the struggle between Eros and Death, between the instincts of life and the instincts of destruction, as it works itself out in the human species."[19]

For all the enormous differences in outlook and insight between the Freudians and the behaviorists, their approaches would seem to converge at one crucial point of "philosophical anthropology"; i.e., both schools share a view of man as essentially the victim-spectator (to use Allport's phrase) of blind forces working through him, whether from without (behaviorism) or from within (instinctivism). Man is thus in the end a passive and reactive structure, a neutral agent, rather than one self-activating and self-actualizing. It is his past condition and conditioning that pushes him; not a vision of possibility that pulls him. He never (almost never?) lives his own life; instead his life lives him.

If this has been the dominant motif in the house that Freud built, however, that paternal mansion has many rooms. Despite the firmness and authority of the orthodox Freudian interpretation—or perhaps because of it—there have been an astonishing number of dissenters and defectors. The first to depart the movement, only a decade after its inception, was Alfred Adler. A year or two later came the desertion of Carl Jung; then of Wilhelm Stekel; then, at approximately five-year intervals, the painful breaks with the master of Otto Rank and Sandor Ferenczi. Although each of these theorists developed his own highly individual approaches and therapeutic methods, they also shared certain common denominators which distinguished them all from Freud. Chief among these were their objections to Freud's psychogenetic reduction of all experience and activity to "a moment in its source," the exclusively sexual derivation of his theory of neurosis, the mechanistic framework of his explanations, and the concentration upon symptoms at the expense of any recognition of the "whole patient."

More important still was the common emphasis of the Freudian heretics upon the constructive possibilities of mind and personality—their reinstatement of consciousness, purpose, life style, and "intentionality" as significant aspects of human experience and behavior. "The most important question of the healthy and diseased mind," wrote Adler, "is not whence? but whither? Only when we know the active, directive goal of a person may we undertake to understand his movements."[20] To which Jung added that the ultimate purpose of psychoanalysis must be "the restoration of the total personality, . . . the bringing into reality of the whole human being—that is, individuation."[21]

This constructive and broadly affirmative approach to the study of lives was carried further by the "second generation" of psychoanalytic theorists both in Europe and America—the so-called neo-Freudians, led by Erich Fromm, Karen Horney, Harry Stack Sullivan, Frieda Fromm-Reichmann, Franz Alexander, Erik Homburger Erikson, and others. The holistic orientation, which someone has labeled "psycho-synthesis" to distinguish it from classical psychoanalysis, has infiltrated the ranks of Freudian orthodoxy in the form of Heinz Hartmahn's ego analysis, which gives to the conscious mind a much more active and autonomous role in behavior than Freud had permitted.[22] What is of most significance, however, is the flourishing development over recent years of that affirmative countermovement of humanistic psychology which regards itself as a "Third Force" standing between the poles of behaviorism and Freudianism. At the hands of such diverse but congenial exponents as Abraham Maslow, Carl R. Rogers, Gordon W. Allport, Gardner Murphy, Rollo May,

Charlotte Buhler, Hadley Cantril, Clark Moustakas, and a growing body of colleagues, the humanistic movement may be said to have emerged from the status of an underground cabal and to have taken its place as a legitimate and hopeful feature of the permanent landscape of psychology.

NOTES

[1]Gordon W. Allport, *Becoming: Basic Considerations for a Psychology of Personality* (New Haven: Yale University Press, 1955), p. 5.

[2]For a particularly illuminating and authoritative account of the Socratic mission, see Werner Jaeger, *Paideia: The Ideals of Greek Culture* (New York: Oxford University Press, 1944), Vol. II.

[3]John B. Watson, *Behaviorism* (Chicago: University of Chicago Press, 1958), pp. 5–6. Watson's book was originally published in 1924.

[4]Jacques Barzun, *Science: The Glorious Entertainment* (New York: Harper and Row, 1964). Cf. Arthur Koestler, *The Sleepwalkers* (New York: Macmillan, 1959); Michael Polanyi, *Personal Knowledge* (Chicago: University of Chicago Press, 1958); Loren Eiseley, *The Firmament of Time* (New York: Atheneum, 1960); W. I. B. Beveridge, *The Art of Scientific Investigation* (New York: Norton, n. d.).

[5]See, in this connection, the remarkable volume by the mathematician and philosopher Anatol Rapoport, *Strategy and Conscience* (New York: Harper and Row, 1964). Cf. Norbert Wiener, *The Human Use of Human Beings* (Garden City: Doubleday Anchor, 1954), pp. 180–186.

[6]P. W. Bridgman, *The Way Things Are* (New York: Viking, 1961 edition), p. 6. Cf. Bridgman, *Reflections of a Physicist* (New York: Philosophical Library, 1950), pp. 372–373.

[7]On the first of these reductions, the classic statement is Harry Stack Sullivan, *The Interpersonal Theory of Psychiatry* (New York: Norton, 1953). The second reduction, which views society as no more than the sum of its individual parts, constitutes the occupational bias usually described as "psychologism"—attributed to psychologists who allegedly cannot see the social forest for the particulate human trees. See, for example, Bernard Rosenberg, Israel Gerver, and F. William Howton (eds.), *Mass Society in Crisis* (New York: Macmillan, 1964), chap. 3, "Psychologism."

[8]Cf. for detailed reinforcements of this claim, Abraham H. Maslow, *Toward a Psychology of Being* (Princeton: Van Nostrand, 1962); Maslow, *The Psychology of Science: A Reconnaissance* (New York: Harper and Row, 1966); Gordon W. Allport, *Personality and Social Encounter* (Boston: Beacon, 1960); Carl R. Rogers, *On Becoming a Person* (New York: Houghton Mifflin, 1961); Floyd W. Matson, *The Broken Image: Man, Science and Society* (New York: Braziller, 1964).

[9]See James F. T. Bugental (ed.), *The Challenge of Humanistic Psychology* (New York: McGraw-Hill, 1967); Francis T. Severin (ed.), *Humanistic Viewpoints in Psychology* (New York: McGraw-Hill, 1965); Charlotte Buhler, *Values in Psychotherapy* (New York: Free Press, 1962); Ernest Becker, *The Revolution in Psychiatry* (New York: Free Press, 1964); James F. T. Bugental, *The Search for Authenticity* (New York: Holt, Rinehart and Winston, 1965). Cf. the *Journal of Humanistic Psychology*, since 1961 a quarterly publication of the American Association for Humanistic Psychology.

10James first dealt with this distinction, in terms of the difference between objective and subjective perspectives, in *The Varieties of Religious Experience* (1903), and subsequently pursued the matter in his *Pragmatism* (1907). For a recent adaptation of this scheme, see Heinz and Rowena Ansbacher, *The Individual Psychology of Alfred Adler* (New York: Basic Books, 1956), Introduction.

11Plato, *Phaedo*, in *Great Dialogues of Plato* (New York: Mentor, 1956).

12See Philip Rieff, *Freud: The Mind of the Moralist* (New York: Viking, 1959), chap. X, "The Emergence of Psychological Man."

13Prominent examples include Gilbert Ryle, *The Concept of Mind* (London: Hutchinson, 1949); Jean-Paul Sartre, *The Transcendence of the Ego: An Existentialist Theory of Consciousness* (New York: Noonday Press, 1957); Ernst Cassirer, *An Essay on Man* (New York: Doubleday Anchor, 1953).

14Warner Fite, *The Living Mind* (New York: Dial Press, 1930), p. 34.

15Michael Polanyi, *The Logic of Liberty* (Chicago: University of Chicago Press, 1951), p. 22. Cf. Donald Snygg and A. W. Combs, *Individual Behavior* (New York: Harper, 1949), p. 24n.

16Friedrich Heer, *The Medieval World* (Cleveland and New York: World, 1962), pp. 215–216.

17E. A. Burtt, *The Metaphysical Foundations of Modern Science* (Garden City: Doubleday Anchor, 1955), pp. 238–239.

18That this is not a peculiarity of Skinner's novel but is rather the consistent expression of the author's scientific metaphysics is made emphatically clear in his other writings, notably *Science and Human Behavior* (New York: Macmillan, 1953), from which the selection by Skinner in the present volume, "The Problem of Control," has been excerpted. Cf. Skinner, "The Control of Human Behavior," *Transactions of the New York Academy of Sciences*, Ser. II, XVII (May, 1955).

19Sigmund Freud, *Civilization and Its Discontents* (London: Hogarth Press and the Institute of Psychoanalysis, Third Edition, 1946), pp. 102–103.

20Alfred Adler, *The Practice and Theory of Individual Psychology* (New York: Harcourt, Brace, 1927), p. 244.

21C. G. Jung, *Modern Man in Search of a Soul* (New York: Harcourt, Brace Harvest Books, 1960), p. 26.

22See Hartmann's paper, "Ego Psychology and the Problem of Adaptation," first published in 1939 and reprinted in David Rapoport, *Organization and Pathology of Thought* (New York: Columbia University Press, 1951), pp. 383 *et seq*. Cf. David Rapoport, "The Autonomy of the Ego," in R. P. Knight and C. R. Friedman, *Psychoanalytic Psychiatry and Psychology* (New York: International Universities Press, 1954).

PART I ooo

The Foundations:

Psychology as Philosophy

Aristotle (384–322 B.C.)

Early Theories of the Soul

Known as the Great Realist, Aristotle wrote what is probably the first textbook in psychology, a work at once historical and systematically analytic: *De Anima*. Influenced by his earlier scientific training (his father was a court physician), Aristotle regarded mind as very much a part of nature; however, his concept of "nature" was not static but evolutionary in its ascending hierarchy of objects and organisms. At the summit is the psyche or soul, which in turn is seen to possess three levels or stages of development. The first of these stages, the *vegetative* soul, characterizes the world of plants, which display only the functions of growth and nutrition. The second stage, the *sensitive* soul, is represented by animals, which possess the additional functions of sensitivity, locomotion, impulse, "imagination" (retention of past impressions), and rudimentary reasoning ability. Man alone possesses the third psychic quality, the *rational* soul—the capacity for thinking. Interestingly, Aristotle's conception of reason went beyond his generally biological orientation; although he declared that all of knowledge is furnished by the senses, and would therefore seem to be in the company of the later empiricists such as Locke, Aristotle was not content to leave the human mind or psyche in a state of passive dependence upon impinging stimuli. Instead he divided human reason into a *passive* and an *active* force, the latter described (in much the

23

same language as his mentor Plato) as "transcendental and immortal."

The following selection, taken from *De Anima*, presents a historical account of the psychological—or, more accurately, the psychic—speculations of earlier Greek physicists and philosophers, from the pre-Socratic thinkers up to and including the theories of Plato concerning the soul.

IN OUR ENQUIRY CONCERNING soul it is necessary to state the problems which must be solved as we proceed, and at the same time to collect the views of our predecessors who had anything to say on the subject, in order that we may adopt what is right in their conclusions and guard against their mistakes. Our enquiry will begin by presenting what are commonly held to be in a special degree the natural attributes of soul. Now there are two points especially wherein that which is animate is held to differ from the inanimate, namely, motion and the act of sensation: and these are approximately the two characteristics of soul handed down to us by our predecessors. There are some who maintain that soul is pre-eminently and primarily the cause of movement. But they imagined that that which is not itself in motion cannot move anything else, and thus they regarded the soul as a thing which is in motion. Hence Democritus affirms the soul to be a sort of fire or heat. For the "shapes" or atoms are infinite and those which are spherical he declares to be fire and soul: they may be compared with the so-called motes in the air, which are seen in the sunbeams that enter through our windows. The aggregate of such seeds, he tells us, forms the constituent elements of the whole of nature (and herein he agrees with Leucippus), while those of them which are spherical form the soul, because such figures most easily find their way through everything and, being themselves in motion, set other things in motion. The atomists assume that it is the soul which imparts motion to animals. It is for this reason that they make life depend upon respiration. For, when the surrounding air presses upon bodies and tends to extrude those atomic shapes which, because they are never at rest themselves, impart motion to animals, then they are reinforced from outside by the entry of other like atoms in respiration, which in fact, by helping to check compression and solidification, prevent the escape of the atoms already contained in the animals; and life, so they hold, continues so long as there is strength to do this. The doctrine of the Pythagoreans seems also to contain the same thought. Some of them identified soul with the motes in the air, others with that which sets these motes in motion: and as to these motes it has been stated that they are seen to be in incessant motion, even though there be a perfect calm. The view of others who describe the soul as that which moves itself tends in the same direction. For it would seem that all these thinkers regard motion as the most distinctive characteristic of the soul. Everything else, they think, is moved by the soul, but the soul is moved by itself: and this because they never see anything cause motion without itself being in motion. Similarly the soul is said to be the moving principle by Anaxagoras and all others who have held that mind sets the universe in motion; but not altogether in the same sense as by Democritus. The latter, indeed, absolutely identified soul and kind, holding that the presentation to the senses is the truth: hence, he observed, Homer had well sung of Hector in his swoon that he lay "with other thoughts." Democritus, then, does not use the term mind to denote a faculty conversant with truth, but regards mind as identical with soul. Anaxagoras, however, is less exact in his use of the terms. In many places he speaks of mind as the cause of goodness and order, but elsewhere he identifies it with the soul: as where he attributes it to all animals, both great and small, high and low. As a matter of fact, however, mind in the sense of intelligence would not seem to be present in all animals alike, nor even in all men.

Those, then, who have directed their attention to the motion of the animate being, conceived the soul as that which is most capable of causing motion: while those who laid stress on its knowledge and perception of all that exists identified the soul with the ultimate principles, whether they recognized a plurality of these or only one. Thus Empedocles compounded soul out of all the elements, while at the same time regarding each one of them as a soul. His words are "With earth we see earth, with water water, with air bright air, but ravaging fire by fire, love by love, and strife by gruesome strife." In the same manner Plato in the *Timaeus* constructs the soul out of the elements. Like, he there maintains, is known by like, and the things we know are composed of the ultimate principles. In like manner it was explained in the lectures on philosophy, that the self-animal or universe is made up of the idea of One, and of the idea-numbers Two, or primary length, Three, primary breadth, and Four, primary depth, and similarly with all the rest of the ideas. And again this has been put in another way as follows: reason is the One, knowledge is the Two, because it proceeds by a single road to one conclusion, opinion is the number of a surface, Three, and sensation the number of a solid, Four. In fact, according to them the numbers, though they are the ideas themselves, or the ultimate principles, are nevertheless derived from elements. And things are judged, some by reason, others by knowledge, others again by opinion and others by sensation: while these idea-numbers are forms of things. And since the soul was held to be thus cognitive as well as capable of causing motion, some thinkers have combined the two and defined the soul as a self-moving number.

But there are differences of opinion as to the nature and number of the ultimate principles, especially between those thinkers who make the principles corporeal and those who make them incorporeal; and again between both of these and others who combine the two and take their principles from both. But, further, they differ also as to their number: some assuming a single principle, some a plurality. And, when they come to give an account of the soul, they do so in strict accordance with their several views. For they have assumed, not unnaturally, that the soul is that primary cause which in its own nature is capable of producing motion. And this is why some identified soul with fire, this being the element which is made up of the finest particles and is most nearly incorporeal, while further it is pre-eminently an element which both moves and sets other things in motion. Democritus has expressed more neatly the reason for each of these facts. Soul he regards as identical with mind, and this he makes to consist of the primary indivisible bodies and considers it to be a cause of motion from the fineness of its particles and their shape. Now the shape which is most susceptible of motion is the spherical; and of atoms of this shape mind, like fire, consists. Anaxagoras, while apparently understanding by mind something different from soul, as we remarked above, really treats both as a single nature, except that it is pre-eminently mind which he takes as his first principle; he says at any rate that mind alone of things that exist is simple, unmixed, pure. But he refers both knowledge and motion to the same principle, when he says that mind sets the universe in motion. Thales, too, apparently, judging from the anecdotes related of him, conceived soul as a cause of motion, if it be true that he affirmed the loadstone to possess soul, because it attracts iron. Diogenes, however, as also some others, identified soul with air. Air, they thought, is made up of the finest particles and is the first principle: and this explains the fact that the soul knows and is a cause of motion, knowing by virtue of being the primary element from which all else is derived, and causing motion by the extreme fineness of its parts. Heraclitus takes soul for his first principle, as he identifies it with the vapour from which he derives all other things, and further says that it is the least corporeal of things and in ceaseless flux; and that it is by something in motion that what is in motion is known; for he, like most philosophers, conceived all that exists to be in motion. Alcmaeon, too, seems to have had a similar conception. For soul, he maintains, is immortal because it is like the beings which are immortal; and it has this attribute in virtue of being ever in motion: for he attributes continuous and unending motion to everything which is divine, moon, sun, stars and the whole heaven. Among cruder thinkers there have been some like Hippon, who have even asserted the soul to be water. The reason for this view seems to have been the fact that in all animals the seed is moist: in fact, Hippon refutes those who make the soul to be blood by pointing out that the seed is not blood, and that this seed is the rudimentary soul. Others, again, like Critias, maintain the soul to be blood, holding that it is sentience which is most distinctive of soul and that this is due to the nature of blood. Thus each of the four elements except earth has found its supporter. Earth, however, has not been put forward by anyone, except by those who have explained the soul to be derived from, or identical with, all the elements.

Thus practically all define the soul by three characteristics, motion, perception and incorporeality; and each of these characteristics is referred to the ultimate principles. Hence all who define soul by its capacity for knowledge either make it an element or derive it from the elements, being on this point, with one exception, in general agreement. Like, they tell us, is known by like; and therefore, since the soul knows all things, they say it consists of all the ultimate principles. Thus those thinkers who admit only one cause and one element, as fire or air, assume the soul also to be one element; while those who admit a plurality of principles assume plurality also in the soul. Anaxagoras alone says that mind cannot be acted upon and has nothing in common with any other thing. How, if such be its nature, it will know anything and how its knowledge is to be explained, he has omitted to state; nor do his utterances afford a clue. All those who introduce pairs of opposites among their principles make the soul also to consist of opposites; while those who take one or other of the two opposites, either hot or cold or something else of the sort, reduce the soul also to one or other of these elements. Hence, too, they etymologise according to their theories; some identify soul with heat, deriving ζῆν from ζεῖν, and contend that this identity accounts for the word for life; others say that what is cold is called soul from the respiratory process and consequent "cooling down," deriving ψυχή from ψύχειν. Such, then, are the views regarding soul which have come down to us and the grounds on which they are held.

Lucretius (c. 96–55 B.C.)

The Mind

The great disciple of Epicurus (who had lived two centuries earlier) was a Roman poet whose celebration of the life of reason was ironically betrayed in his own life by the advent of insanity and ultimately of suicide. Nevertheless, his epic work, *De Rerum Natura* (On the Nature of Things), remains the definitive expression of the Epicurean philosophy of the transcendence of human reason and will over necessity, sensuality, and superstition. Although he was a materialist in his reliance upon the atomistic philosophy of Democritus and in his denial of the existence of an immortal soul, Lucretius was an "existentialist" in his insistence upon the power of independent reason to pursue happiness and to overcome the adversities of fate.

The present selection is taken from the third book (on the mind) of the six-book *De Rerum Natura*, a poetic argument concerning the nature of all things, human and natural, which combines dignity and passion in its strikingly "modern" approach to the science of mind and the meaning of existence.

FIRST THEN I SAY that the mind which we often call the understanding, in which dwells the directing and governing principle of life, is no less part of the man, than hand and foot and eyes are parts of the whole living creature. [Some however affirm] that the sense of the mind does not dwell in a distinct part, but is a certain vital state of the body, which the Greeks call harmonia, because by it, they say, we live with sense, though the understanding is in no one part; just as when good health is said to belong to the body, though yet it is not any one part of the man in health. In this way they do not assign a distinct part to the sense of the mind; in all which they appear to me to be grievously at fault in more ways than one. Oftentimes the body which is visible to sight, is sick, while yet we have pleasure in another hidden part; and oftentimes the case is the very reverse, the man who is unhappy in mind feeling pleasure in his whole body; just as if, while a sick man's foot is pained, the head meanwhile should be in no pain at all. Moreover when the limbs are consigned to soft sleep and the burdened body lies diffused without sense, there is yet a something else in us which during that time is moved in many ways and admits into it all the motions of joy and unreal cares of the heart. Now that you may know that the soul as well is in the limbs and that the body is not wont to have sense by any harmony, this is a main proof: when much of the body has been taken away, still life often stays in the limbs; and yet the same life, when a few bodies of heat have been dispersed abroad and some air has been forced out through the mouth, abandons at once the veins and quits the bones: by this you may perceive that all bodies have not functions of like importance nor alike uphold existence, but rather that those seeds which constitute wind and heat, cause life to stay in the limbs. Therefore vital heat and wind are within the body and abandon our frame at death. Since then the nature of the mind and that of the soul have been proved to be a part as it were of the man, surrender the name of harmony, whether brought down to musicians from high Helicon, or whether rather they have themselves taken it from something else and transferred it to that thing which then was in need of a distinctive name; whatever it be, let them keep it: do you take in the rest of my precepts.

Now I assert that the mind and the soul are kept together in close union and make up a single nature, but that the directing principle which we call mind and understanding, is the head so to speak and reigns paramount in the whole body. It has a fixed seat in the middle region of the breast: here throb fear and apprehension, about these spots dwell soothing joys; therefore here is the understanding or mind. All the rest of the soul disseminated through the whole body obeys and moves at the will and inclination of the mind. It by itself alone knows for itself, rejoices for itself, at times when the impression does not move either soul or body together with it. And as when some part of us, the head or the eye, suffers from an attack of pain, we do not feel the anguish at the same time over the whole body, thus the mind sometimes suffers pain by itself or is inspirited with joy, when all the rest of the soul throughout the limbs and frame is stirred by no novel sensation. But when the mind is excited by some more vehement apprehension, we see the whole soul feel in unison through all the limbs, sweats and paleness spread over the whole body, the tongue falter, the voice die away, a mist cover the eyes, the ears ring, the limbs sink under one; in short we often see men drop down from terror of mind; so that anybody may easily perceive from this that the soul is closely united with the mind, and, when it has been smitten by the influence of the mind, forthwith pushes and strikes the body.

This same principle teaches that the nature of the mind and soul is bodily; for when it is seen to push the limbs, rouse the body from sleep, and alter the countenance and guide and turn about the whole man, and when we see that none of these effects can take place without touch nor touch without body, must we not admit that the mind and the soul are of a bodily nature? Again you perceive that our mind in our body suffers together with the body and feels in unison with it. When a weapon with a shudder-causing force has been driven in and has laid bare bones and sinews within the body, if it does not take life, yet there ensues a faintness and a lazy sinking to the ground and on the ground the turmoil of mind which arises, and sometimes a kind of undecided inclination to get up. Therefore the nature of the mind must be bodily, since it suffers from bodily weapons and blows.

I will now go on to explain in my verses of what kind of body the mind consists and out of what it is formed. First of all I say that it is extremely fine and formed of exceedingly minute bodies. That this is so you may, if you please to attend, clearly perceive from what follows: nothing that is seen takes place with a velocity equal to that of the mind when it starts some suggestion and actually sets it agoing; the mind therefore is stirred with greater rapidity than any of the things whose nature stands out visible to sight. But that which is so passing nimble, must consist of seeds exceedingly round and exceedingly minute, in order to be stirred and set in motion by a small moving power. Thus water is moved and heaves by ever so small a force, formed as it is of small particles apt to roll. But on the other hand the nature of honey is more sticky, its liquid more sluggish and its movement more dilatory; for the whole mass of matter coheres more closely, because sure enough it is made of bodies not so smooth, fine and round. A breeze however gentle and light can force, as you may see, a high heap of poppy seed to be blown away from the top downwards; but on the other hand eurus itself cannot move a heap of stones. Therefore bodies possess a power of moving in proportion to their smallness and smoothness; and on the other hand the greater weight and roughness bodies prove to have, the more stable they are. Since then the nature of the mind has been found to be eminently easy to move, it must consist of bodies exceedingly small, smooth and round. The knowledge of which fact, my good friend, will on many accounts prove useful and be serviceable to you. The following fact too likewise demonstrates how fine the texture is of which its nature is composed, and how small the room is in which it can be contained, could it only be collected into one mass: soon as the untroubled sleep of death has gotten hold of a man and the nature of the mind and soul has withdrawn, you can perceive then no diminution of the entire body either in appearance or weight: death makes all good save the vital sense and heat. Therefore the whole soul must consist of very small seeds and be inwoven through veins and flesh and sinews; inasmuch as, after it has all withdrawn from the whole body, the exterior contour of the limbs preserves itself entire and not a tittle of the weight is lost. Just in the same way when the flavour of wine is gone or when the delicious aroma of a perfume has been dispersed into the air or when the savour has left some body, yet the thing itself does not therefore look smaller to the eye, nor does aught seem to have been taken from the weight, because sure enough many minute seeds make up the savours and the odour in the whole body of the several things. Therefore, again and again I say, you are to know that the nature of the mind and the soul has been formed of exceedingly minute seeds, since at its departure it takes away none of the weight.

Thomas Hobbes (1588–1679)

Human Nature: The Passions

Hobbes, who gained his reputation as a political philosopher, grounded his authoritarian theory of government (which conceived the ideal state as a "Leviathan" receiving the total allegiance of its subjects) upon a conception of human nature which anticipated Freud in one way and the behaviorist school in another. Man in the "state of nature" was a beast to man, driven primarily by fear and selfishness; his only civilized recourse must be to relinquish the burden of that dreadful freedom by accepting the authority of a sovereign who alone could guarantee security and order.

For Hobbes, "the sole and adequate explanation of the universe is to be found in terms of body and motion." Nor was it only the outer physical world which was reducible to mechanistic materialism; mind and thought together with all human activity were to be accounted for in terms of the motions of an animal organism: "If this be so, reasoning will depend on names, names on the imagination, and imagination, perchance, as I think, on the motion of the corporeal organs. Thus mind will be nothing but the motions in certain parts of an organic body." More significantly, Hobbes contributed to the empiricist theory of association by holding that the "Trayne of Thoughts" or "Mentall Discourse" are copies of past sensations which become associated by being experienced together—a viewpoint soon to be greatly elaborated by Locke, Hume, and others who preferred the doctrine of an "empty organism" to that of an active and intrinsically purposeful intellect. The following selection is taken from Hobbes' *Human Nature, or the Fundamental Elements of Policie.*

1. IN THE EIGHTH SECTION of the second chapter is shewed, *that conceptions* and *apparitions* are nothing *really*, but *motion* in some internal substance of the *head*; which motion *not stopping* there, but proceeding to the *heart*, of necessity must there either *help* or *hinder* the motion which is called *vital*; when it *helpeth*, it is called *delight, contentment*, or *pleasure*, which is nothing really but motion about the heart, as conception is nothing but motion in the head: and the *objects* that cause it are called *pleasant* or *delightful*, or by some name equivalent; the Latins have *jucundum, a juvando*, from helping; and the same delight, with reference to the object, is called *love*: but when such motion *weakeneth* or hindereth the vital motion, then it is called *pain*; and in relation to that which causeth it, hatred, which the Latins express sometimes by *odium*, and sometimes by *taedium*.

2. This motion, in which consisteth *pleasure* or *pain*, is also a *solicitation* or provocation either to draw *near* to the thing that pleaseth, or to *retire* from the thing that displeaseth; and this solicitation is the *endeavor* or internal beginning of *animal* motion, which when the object *delighteth*, is called *appetite*; when it *displeaseth*, it is called *aversion*, in respect of the displeasure *present*; but in respect of the displeasure *expected, fear*. So that, *pleasure, love*, and *appetite*, which is also called desire, are *divers names* for divers considerations of the *same thing*.

3. Every man, for his own part, calleth that which *pleaseth*, and is delightful to himself, *good*; and that *evil* which *displeaseth* him: insomuch that while every man *differeth* from

another in *constitution*, they differ also from one another concerning the common distinction of good and evil. Nor is there any such thing as absolute goodness, considered without relation: for even the goodness which we apprehend in God Almighty, is *his goodness to us*. And as we call *good* and *evil* the *things* that please and displease; so call we *goodness* and *badness*, the *qualities* or powers whereby they do it: and the signs of that goodness are called by the Latins in one word *pulchritudo*, and the signs of evil, *turpitudo*; to which we have no words precisely answerable.

As all conceptions we have immediately by the *sense*, are, *delight*, or *pain*, or *appetite*, or fear; so are all the *imaginations* after sense. But as they are weaker imaginations, so are they also weaker pleasures, or weaker pain.

4. As *appetite* is the beginning of *animal* motion towards something that pleaseth us; so is the *attaining* thereof, the *end* of that motion, which we also call the *scope*, and aim, and final cause of the same: and when we attain that end, the delight we have thereby is called the *fruition*: so that *bonum* and *finis* are different names, but for different considerations of the same thing.

5. And of *ends*, some of them are called *propinqui*, that is, near at hand; others *remoti*, far off: but when the ends that be nearer attaining, be compared with those that be further off, they are called not ends, but *means*, and the *way* to those. But for an *utmost* end, in which the ancient *philosophers* have placed *felicity*, and disputed much concerning the way thereto, there is no such thing in this world, nor way to it, more than to Utopia: for while we live, we have desires, and desire presupposeth a further end. Those things which please us, as the way or *means* to a further end, we call *profitable*; and the *fruition* of them, *use*; and those things that profit not, *vain*.

6. Seeing all *delight* is *appetite*, and presupposeth a *further*

end, there can be *no contentment* but in *proceeding*: and therefore we are not to marvel, when we see, that as men attain to more riches, honour, or other power; so their appetite continually groweth more and more; and when they are come to the utmost degree of some kind of power, they pursue some other, as long as in any kind they think themselves behind any other: of those therefore that have attained to the highest degree of honour and riches, some have affected mastery in some art; as Nero in music and poetry, Commodus in the art of a gladiator; and such as affect not some such thing, must find diversion and recreation of their thoughts in the contention either of play or business: and men justly complain of a great grief, that they know not what to do. *Felicity*, therefore, by which we mean continual delight, consisteth *not* in *having* prospered, but in *prospering*.

7. There are few things in this world, but *either* have *mixture* of good and evil, *or* there is a chain of them so necessarily linked together, that the one cannot be taken without the other: as for example, the pleasures of sin, and the bitterness of punishment, are inseparable; as is also labour and honour, for the most part. Now when in the *whole chain*, the *greater part* is good, the *whole* is called *good*; and when the *evil* over-weigheth, the *whole* is called *evil*.

8. There are two sorts of pleasure, whereof the *one* seemeth to affect the *corporeal* organ of the sense, and that I call *sensual*; the *greatest* part whereof, is that by which we are invited to give continuance to our *species*; and the *next*, by which a man is invited to meat, for the preservation of his *individual* person: the *other sort* of delight is not particular to any part of the body, and is called the delight of the *mind*, and is that which we call *joy*. Likewise of *pains*, some affect the *body*, and are therefore called the *pains* of the body; and some *not*, and those are called *grief*.

René Descartes   (1596–1650)

The Passions of the Soul

Modern science in general, and modern psychology in particular, are customarily said to have begun with Descartes. He was the father of physiological psychology and reflexology as well as the inventor of analytic geometry and the founder of the Cartesian philosophy based upon the dualism of mind and body. Toward matter and the body he was a thoroughgoing mechanist, setting in motion the conception of man as a machine that was to gain its most consistent expression in the work of the eighteenth-century French materialists led by La Mettrie. Descartes' dualism consisted in the assertion of an interaction between the free and insubstantial realm of mind and the mechanically operated body (extended substance). The "unextended soul," as he explained in his major psychological work *Les Passions de l'Âme*, is "all that is in us and which we can not conceive in any manner possible to pertain to a body." It is the soul that perceives and wills, and its interaction with the body occurs at the singular point of the pineal gland, or "conarium."

On a November night in the year 1619, the young Descartes experienced a famous dream which opened up to him the vision of a "Science of Sciences" which would provide the foundation of all human knowledge. The fruit of this dream was the essay for which he is primarily remembered, the *Discourse on Method*, published in 1637. Subjecting everything, including doubt itself, to the test of doubt, Descartes was led to his well-known principle of fundamental certainty: *Cogito, ergo sum*—I think, therefore I am. More importantly, perhaps, Descartes developed in his discourse the geometrical theory of space or extension as the basic reality, with motion as its essential principle and mathematics as the language of its revelation. "Give me extension and motion," he wrote, "and I will construct the universe." The Cartesian universe which he built on those deductive foundations has since been replaced by other structures in philosophy and psychology alike (notably the more empirical theories of associationism and behaviorism), but its influence is still felt in contemporary concepts of dualism, interactionism, and mechanism.

ARTICLE I

Passion, as respects the subject, is always action in some other respect.

There is nothing which better shows how defective the sciences are which we have received from the ancients than what they have written upon the passions; for, although it is a subject the knowledge of which has always been much sought after, and which does not appear to be one of the more difficult sciences, because everyone, feeling the passions in himself, stands in no need whatever of borrowing any observation elsewhere to discover their nature, nevertheless, what the ancients have taught on this subject is of such slight intent, and for the most part so untrustworthy, that I cannot have any hope of reaching the truth, except by abandoning the paths which they have followed. That is the reason why I shall be obliged to write now in the same way as I should if I were treating a topic which no one before me had ever touched upon; and, to begin with, I take into consideration the fact that an event is generally spoken of by philosophers as a passion as regards the subject to which it happens, and an action in respect to that which causes it; so that, although the agent and the patient may often be very different, action and passion are always one and the same thing, which has these two names because of the two different subjects to which it can be referred.

ARTICLE II

In order to understand the passions of the soul, it is necessary to distinguish its functions from those of the body.

Next I take into consideration that we know of no subject which acts more immediately upon our soul than the body to which it is joined, and that consequently we must think that what in the one is a passion is commonly in the other an action; so that there is no better path to the knowledge of our passions than to examine into the difference between the soul and the body, in order to know to which of them is to be attributed each of our functions.

ARTICLE III

The rule to be observed to this end.

No great difficulty will be found in this, if it be borne in mind that all that which we experience in ourselves which we see can also take place in bodies entirely inanimate is to be attributed only to our body; and, on the contrary, all that which is in us and which we cannot conceive in any manner possible to pertain to a body is to be attributed to our soul.

ARTICLE IV

That heat and the movement of the limbs proceed from the body, thoughts from the mind.

Thus, because we cannot conceive that the body thinks in any manner whatever, we have no reason but to think that all forms of thought which are in us belong to the mind; and because we cannot doubt that there are inanimate bodies which can move in as many or more different ways than ours, and which have as much or more heat (as experience teaches us in the case of flame, which alone has more heat and motion than any of our members), we must believe that all the heat and all the motions which are in us, in so far as they do not depend at all on thought, belong only to the body.

ARTICLE V

That it is an error to think that the soul imparts motion and heat to the body.

By this means we shall avoid a very great error, into which many have fallen, an error which I consider to be the principal hindrance, up to the present time, to a correct explanation of the passions and other properties of the soul. It consists in this, that, seeing that all dead bodies are deprived of heat and, consequently, of motion, it is imagined that the absence of the soul causes these movements and this heat to cease; and thus it has been thought, without reason, that our natural heat and all the motions of our body depend upon the soul; instead of which it should be thought, on the contrary, that soul departs, when death occurs, only because this heat fails and the organs which serve to move the body decay.

ARTICLE VI

The difference between a living and a dead body.

In order, then, that we may avoid this error, let us consider that death never takes place through the absence of a soul, but solely because some one of the principal parts of the body has fallen into decay; and let us conclude that the body of a living man differs as much from that of a dead man as does a watch or other automaton (that is to say, or other machine which moves of itself), when it is wound up, and has within itself the material principle of the movements for which it is constructed, with all that is necessary for its action, from the same watch or other machine, when it has been broken, and the principle of its movement ceases to act.

ARTICLE VII

Brief explanation of the parts of the body and of some of its functions.

In order to render this more intelligible, I will explain here in a few words how the entire mechanism of our body is composed. There is no one who does not already know that there is in us a heart, a brain, a stomach, muscles, nerves, arteries, veins, and such things; it is known also that the food we eat descends into the stomach and the bowels, where their juices flowing through the liver and through all the veins, mix themselves with the blood they contain, and by this means increase its quantity. Those who have heard the least talk in medicine know, further, how the heart is constructed, and how all the blood of the veins can easily flow through the *vena cava* on its right side, and thence pass into the lung, by the vessel which is called the arterial vein, then return from the lung on the left side of the heart, by the vessel called the venous artery, and finally pass thence into the great artery, the branches of which are diffused through the whole body. Also, all of those whom the authority of the ancients has not entirely blinded, and who are willing to open their eyes to examine the opinion of Hervaeus in regard to the circulation of the blood, have no doubt whatever that all the veins and arteries of the body are merely channels through which the blood flows without cessation and very rapidly, starting from the right cavity of the heart by the arterial vein, the branches of which are dispersed through-

out the lungs and joined to that of the venous artery, by
which it passes from the lungs into the left side of the heart;
next, from thence it passes into the great artery, the branches
of which, scattered throughout all the rest of the body, are
joined to the branches of the vein, which carry once more
the same blood into the right cavity of the heart; so that
these two cavities are like sluices, through each of which all
the blood passes every time it makes the circuit of the body.
Still further, it is known that all the movements of the limbs
depend upon the muscles, and that these muscles are opposed to one another in such a way that, when one of them
contracts, it draws toward itself the part of the body to which
it is attached, which at the same time stretches out the muscle
which is opposed to it; then, if it happens, at another time,
that this last contracts, it causes the first to lengthen, and
draws toward itself the part to which they are attached.
Finally, it is known that all these movements of the muscles,
as also all the senses, depend upon the nerves, which are like
minute threads, or small tubes, all of which come from the
brain, and contain, like that, a certain subtle air or breath,
which is called the animal spirits.

ARTICLE VIII

The principle of all these functions.

But it is not commonly known in what manner these
animal spirits and these nerves contribute to the movements
of the limbs and to the senses, nor what is the corporeal
principle which makes them act; it is for this reason, although I have already touched upon this matter in other
writings, I shall not omit to say here briefly, that, as long as
we live, there is a continual heat in our heart, which is a
kind of fire kept up there by the blood of the veins, and

that this fire is the corporeal principle of the movements of our limbs. . . .

ARTICLE XVI

How all the limbs can be moved by the objects of the senses and by the spirits without the aid of the soul.

Finally, it is to be observed that the machine of our body is so constructed that all the changes which occur in the motion of the spirits may cause them to open certain pores of the brain rather than others, and, reciprocally, that when any one of these pores is opened in the least degree more or less than is usual by the action of the nerves which serve the senses, this changes somewhat the motion of the spirits, and causes them to be conducted into the muscles which serve to move the body in the way in which it is commonly moved on occasion of such action; so that all the movements which we make without our will contributing thereto (as frequently happens when we breathe, or walk, or eat, and, in fine, perform all those actions which are common to us and the brutes) depend only on the conformation of our limbs and the course which the spirits, excited by the heat of the heart, naturally follow in the brain, in the nerves, and in the muscles, in the same way that the movement of a watch is produced by the force solely of its mainspring and the form of its wheels. . . .

ARTICLE XXX

That the soul is united to all parts of the body conjointly.

But, in order to understand all these things more perfectly, it is necessary to know that the soul is truly joined to the entire body, and that it cannot properly be said to be in any one of its parts to the exclusion of the rest, because the body is one, and in a manner indivisible, on account of the arrangement of its organs, which are so related to one another, that when any one of them is taken away, that makes the whole body defective: and because the soul is of a nature which has no relation to extension, or to dimensions, or other properties of the matter of which the body is composed, but solely to the whole collection of its organs, as appears from the fact that we cannot at all conceive of the half or the third of a soul, nor what space it occupies, and that it does not become any smaller when any part of the body is cut off, but that it separates itself entirely from it when the combination of its organs is broken up.

John Locke (1632–1704)

Of Ideas in General

"Virtually all modern psychological theories," according to Gordon W. Allport, "seem oriented toward one of two polar conceptions, which . . . I shall call the Lockean and Leibnitzian traditions respectively."* The contrast which Allport wished to call attention to was that between "their views on one aspect of man's mind—its essentially passive nature (Locke) or its active nature (Leibnitz)." For Locke, the first of the great trio of British empiricists and father of associationist psychology, the mind of man at birth was a *tabula rasa*, a passive and empty thing awaiting the prick of sensation and the cumulative prods of association in order to take on structure and content. It was this view of man as an essentially *re*active being which Allport has regarded as contrasting strikingly with the Leibnitzian conception of the active human mind going out to meet the world and to shape it according to inherent propensities and creative purposes.

Locke's greatest work, the *Essay Concerning Human Understanding*, from which the present excerpt is taken, was published in 1690 when its author was fifty-seven years old. It was the outgrowth of an effort at explanation which had begun twenty years before: In order to comprehend the difficulties encountered in discussions of religion and morality, Locke had decided to undertake a criticism of human understanding itself—a work which he at first con-

*Gordon W. Allport, *Becoming* (New Haven: Yale University Press, 1955), p. 7.

sidered might occupy a single sheet of paper. One of the
principal objects of Locke's criticism was the Cartesian
doctrine of innate ideas, to which he opposed the theory of
ideas as the product of experience—as the response to
stimuli from the outer world. His stimulus-response psychology, with its discussion of primary and secondary qualities, its preference for the molecular as against the molar
dimension ("simple ideas" were superior to "complex
ideas"), and its implicit theory of learning as conditioning
and reinforcement of stimuli and responses, became, in
these and other emphases, the precedent and predecessor
of much later psychological theory laying claim to scientific status. Thus Allport concludes that "the Lockean point
of view . . . has been and is still dominant in Anglo-
American psychology. Its representatives are found in associationism of all types, including environmentalism, behaviorism, stimulus-response (familiarly abbreviated as
S-R) psychology, and all other stimulus-oriented psychologies, in animal and genetic psychology, in positivism and
operationism, in mathematical models—in short, in most
of what today is cherished in our laboratories as truly
'scientific' psychology."*

OF IDEAS IN GENERAL, AND THEIR ORIGINAL

1. *Idea is the object of thinking.*—Every man being conscious of himself, that he thinks, and that which his mind
is applied about, whilst thinking, being the ideas that are
there, it is past doubt that men have in their mind several
ideas, such as are those expressed by the words, whiteness,
hardness, sweetness, thinking, motion, man, elephant, army,
drunkenness, and others: it is in the first place then to be
inquired, How he comes by them? I know it is a received

Ibid., p. 8.

doctrine, that men have native ideas and original characters stamped upon their minds in their very first being. This opinion I have at large examined already; and, I suppose, what I have said in the foregoing book will be much more easily admitted, when I have shown whence the understanding may get all the ideas it has, and by what ways and degrees they may come into the mind; for which I shall appeal to every one's own observation and experience.

2. *All ideas come from sensation or reflection.*—Let us then suppose the mind to be, as we say, white paper, void of all characters, without any ideas: How comes it to be furnished? Whence comes it by that vast store, which the busy and boundless fancy of man has painted on it with an almost endless variety? Whence has it all the materials of reason and knowledge? To this I answer, in one word, From *experience.* In that all our knowledge is founded, and from that it ultimately derives itself. Our observation, employed either about external sensible objects, or about the internal operations of our mind, perceived and reflected on by ourselves, is that which supplies our understandings with all the materials of thinking. These two are the fountains of knowledge, from whence all the ideas we have, or can naturally have, do spring.

3. *The object of sensation one source of ideas.*—First. Our senses, conversant about particular sensible objects, do convey into the mind several distinct perceptions of things, according to those various ways wherein those objects do affect them; and thus we come by those ideas we have of yellow, white, heat, cold, soft, hard, bitter, sweet, and all those which we call sensible qualities; which when I say the senses convey into the mind, I mean, they from external objects convey into the mind what produces there those perceptions. This great source of most of the ideas we have,

depending wholly upon our senses, and derived by them to the understanding, I call, SENSATION.

4. *The operations of our minds the other source of them.*— Secondly. The other fountain, from which experience furnisheth the understanding with ideas, is the perception of the operations of our own minds within us, as it is employed about the ideas it has got; which operations when the soul comes to reflect on and consider, do furnish the understanding with another set of ideas which could not be had from things without; and such are perception, thinking, doubting, believing, reasoning, knowing, willing, and all the different actings of our own minds; which we, being conscious of, and observing in ourselves, do from these receive into our understanding as distinct ideas, as we do from bodies affecting our senses. This source of ideas every man has wholly in himself; and though it be not sense as having nothing to do with external objects, yet it is very like it, and might properly enough be called *internal sense*. But as I call the other *sensation*, so I call this REFLECTION, the ideas it affords being such only as the mind gets by reflecting on its own operations within itself. By reflection, then, in the following part of this discourse, I would be understood to mean that notice which the mind takes of its own operations, and the manner of them, by reason whereof there come to be ideas of these operations in the understanding. These two, I say, viz., external material things as the objects of sensation, and the operations of our own minds within as the objects of reflection, are, to me, the only originals from whence all our ideas take their beginnings. The term *operations* here, I use in a large sense, as comprehending not barely the actions of the mind about its ideas, but some sort of passions arising sometimes from them, such as is the satisfaction or uneasiness arising from any thought.

5. *All our ideas are of the one or the other of these.*—The understanding seems to me not to have the least glimmering of any ideas which it doth not receive from one of these two. External objects furnish the mind with the ideas of sensible qualities, which are all those different perceptions they produce in us; and the mind furnishes the understanding with ideas of its own operations.

These, when we have taken a full survey of them, and their several modes [combinations, and relations], we shall find to contain all our whole stock of ideas; and that we have nothing in our minds which did not come in one of these two ways. Let any one examine his own thoughts, and thoroughly search into his understanding, and then let him tell me, whether all the original ideas he has there, are any other than of the objects of his senses, or of the operations of his mind considered as objects of his reflection; and how great a mass of knowledge soever he imagines to be lodged there, he will, upon taking a strict view, see that he has not any idea in his mind but what one of these two have imprinted, though perhaps with infinite variety compounded and enlarged by the understanding, as we shall see hereafter.

.   .   .

OF SIMPLE IDEAS

1. *Uncompounded appearances.*—The better to understand the nature, manner, and extent of our knowledge, one thing is carefully to be observed concerning the ideas we have; and that is, that some of them are *simple*, and some *complex*.

Though the qualities that affect our senses are, in the things themselves, so united and blended that there is no separation, no distance between them; yet it is plain the ideas they produce in the mind enter by the senses simple and unmixed. For though the sight and touch often take in from the same object, at the same time, different ideas—as a man sees at once motion and colour, the hand feels softness and warmth in the same piece of wax—yet the simple ideas thus united in the same subject are as perfectly distinct as those that come in by different senses; the coldness and hardness which a man feels in a piece of ice being as distinct ideas in the mind as the smell and whiteness of a lily, or as the taste of sugar and smell of a rose: and there is nothing can be plainer to a man than the clear and distinct perception he has of those simple ideas; which, being each in itself uncompounded, contains in it nothing but one uniform appearance or conception in the mind, and is not distinguishable into different ideas.

2. *The mind can neither make nor destroy them.*—These simple ideas, the materials of all our knowledge, are suggested and furnished to the mind only by those two ways above mentioned, viz., sensation and reflection. When the understanding is once stored with these simple ideas, it has the power to repeat, compare, and unite them, even to an almost infinite variety, and so can make at pleasure new complex ideas. But it is not in the power of the most exalted wit or enlarged understanding, by any quickness or variety of thought, to invent or frame one new simple idea in the mind, not taken in by the ways before mentioned; nor can any force of the understanding destroy those that are there: the dominion of man in this little world of his own understanding, being much-what the same as it is in the great world of visible things, wherein his power, however managed by art and skill, reaches no farther than to compound and divide the materials that are made to his hand but can do nothing towards the making the least particle of new matter, or destroying one atom of what is already in being. . . .

PART II ooo

The Measure of Mind:

Psychology as Experimental Science

Julien de la Mettrie (1709–1751)

Man—A Machine

Where Descartes left off in his effort to reduce the world and man to the dimensions of mechanism, his later countryman La Mettrie began. For La Mettrie and a few of his Enlightenment colleagues in philosophical psychology (notably Baron d'Holbach), man was a machine and nothing but a machine—with no exemptions or qualifications allowed for the mind or soul. The human organism was to be regarded as a kind of wind-up clock, so ingeniously engineered that if one of its hands should break down the other hand would carry on in its mechanical orbit. For a full explanation of human behavior all that was needed was a knowledge of the clockwork. "If man believes himself free," said Holbach, "he is merely exhibiting a dangerous delusion and an intellectual weakness. It is the structure of the atoms that forms him, and their motion propels him forward; conditions not dependent on him determine his nature and direct his fate."*

It is a suggestive commentary on the ethical implications of this thoroughgoing materialistic determinism that La Mettrie in his later years developed a doctrine of hedonism which argued that pleasure is the goal of life and that all human motivation is fundamentally selfish. And it is an ironic twist that he should have died, only forty-one years

---

*Ernst Cassirer, *The Philosophy of the Enlightenment* (Boston: Beacon Press, 1955), p. 69.

old, at the court of Frederick the Great shortly after dining
on a spoiled game pie—thus encouraging the legend that
he had eaten himself to death.

SINCE ALL THE FACULTIES of the soul depend to such a degree
on the proper organization of the brain and of the whole
body, that apparently they are but this organization itself,
the soul is clearly an enlightened machine. For finally, even
if man alone had received a share of natural law, would he
be any less a machine for that? A few more wheels, a few
more springs than in the most perfect animals, the brain
proportionally nearer the heart and for this very reason receiving more blood—any one of a number of unknown causes
might always produce this delicate conscience so easily
wounded, this remorse which is no more foreign to matter
than to thought, and in a word all the differences that are
supposed to exist here. Could the organism then suffice for
everything? Once more, yes; since thought visibly develops
with our organs, why should not the matter of which they
are composed be susceptible of remorse also, when once it
has acquired, with time, the faculty of feeling?

The soul is therefore but an empty word, of which no
one has any idea, and which an enlightened man should use
only to signify the part in us that thinks. Given the least
principle of motion, animated bodies will have all that is
necessary for moving, feeling, thinking, repenting, or in a
word for conducting themselves in the physical realm, and
in the moral realm which depends upon it.

Yet we take nothing for granted; those who perhaps think
that all the difficulties have not yet been removed shall now
read of experiments that will completely satisfy them.

1. The flesh of all animals palpitates after death. This palpitation continues longer, the more cold blooded the animal is and the less it perspires. Tortoises, lizards, serpents, etc., are evidence of this.

2. Muscles separated from the body contract when they are stimulated.

3. The intestines keep up their peristaltic or vermicular motion for a long time.

4. According to Cowper, a simple injection of hot water reanimates the heart and the muscles.

5. A frog's heart moves for an hour or more after it has been removed from the body, especially when exposed to the sun or better still when placed on a hot table or chair. If this movement seems totally lost, one has only to stimulate the heart, and that hollow muscle beats again. Harvey made this same observation on toads.

6. Bacon of Verulam in his treatise "Sylva Sylvarum" cites the case of a man convicted of treason, who was opened alive, and whose heart thrown into hot water leaped several times, each time less high, to the perpendicular height of two feet.

7. Take a tiny chicken still in the egg, cut out the heart and you will observe the same phenomenon as before, under almost the same conditions. The warmth of the breath alone reanimates an animal about to perish in the air pump.

. . .

9. A drunken soldier cut off with one stroke of his sabre an Indian rooster's head. The animal remained standing, then walked, and ran: happening to run against a wall, it turned around, beat its wings still running, and finally fell down. As it lay on the ground, all the muscles of this rooster

kept on moving. That is what I saw myself, and almost the same phenomena can easily be observed in kittens or puppies with their heads cut off.

10. Polyps do more than move after they have been cut in pieces. In a week they regenerate to form as many animals as there are pieces. I am sorry that these facts speak against the naturalists' system of generation: or rather I am very glad of it, for let this discovery teach us never to reach a general conclusion even on the ground of all known (and most decisive) experiments.

Here we have many more facts than are needed to prove, in an incontestable way, that each tiny fibre or part of an organized body moves by a principle which belongs to it. Its activity, unlike voluntary motions, does not depend in any way on the nerves, since the movements in question occur in parts of the body which have no connection with the circulation. But if this force is manifested even in sections of fibres the heart, which is a composite of peculiarly connected fibres, must possess the same property. I did not need Bacon's story to persuade me of this. It was easy for me to come to this conclusion, both from the perfect analogy of the structure of the human heart with that of animals, and also from the very bulk of the human heart, in which this movement escapes our eyes only because it is smothered, and finally because in corpses all the organs are cold and lifeless. If executed criminals were dissected while their bodies are still warm, we should probably see in their hearts the same movements that are observed in the face-muscles of those that have been beheaded.

The motive principle of the whole body, and even of its parts cut in pieces, is such that it produces not irregular movements, as some have thought, but very regular ones, in warm blooded and perfect animals as well as in cold and imperfect ones. No resource therefore remains open to our adversaries but to deny thousands and thousands of facts which every man can easily verify.

.   .   .

Let us now go into some detail concerning these springs of the human machine. All the vital, animal, natural, and automatic motions are carried on by their action. Is it not in a purely mechanical way that the body shrinks back when it is struck with terror at the sight of an unforeseen precipice, that the eyelids are lowered at the menace of a blow, as some have remarked, and that the pupil contracts in broad daylight to save the retina, and dilates to see objects in darkness? Is it not by mechanical means that the pores of the skin close in winter so that the cold can not penetrate to the interior of the blood vessels, and that the stomach vomits when it is irritated by poison, by a certain quantity of opium and by all emetics, etc.? that the heart, the arteries and the muscles contract in sleep as well as in waking hours, that the lungs serve as bellows continually in exercise,—that the heart contracts more strongly than any other muscle? . . .

I shall not go into any more detail concerning all these little subordinate forces, well known to all. But there is another more subtle and marvelous force, which animates them all; it is the source of all our feelings, of all our pleasures, of all our passions, and of all our thoughts: for the brain has its muscles for thinking, as the legs have muscles for walking. I wish to speak of this impetuous principle that Hippocrates calls *enormon* (soul). This principle exists and has its seat in the brain at the origin of the nerves, by which it exercises its control over all the rest of the body. By this fact is explained all that can be explained, even to the surprising effects of maladies of the imagination. . . .

Look at the portrait of the famous Pope who is, to say the least, the Voltaire of the English. The effort, the energy of his genius are imprinted upon his countenance. It is convulsed. His eyes protrude from their sockets, the eyebrows are raised with the muscles of the forehead. Why? Because the brain is in travail and all the body must share in such a laborious deliverance. If there were not an internal cord which pulled the external ones, whence could come all these phenomena? To admit a soul as explanation of them, is to be reduced to [explaining phenomena by] the operations of the Holy Spirit.

In fact, if what thinks in my brain is not a part of this organ and therefore of the whole body, why does my blood boil, and the fever of my mind pass into my veins, when lying quietly in bed? I am forming the plan of some work or carrying on an abstract calculation. Put this question to men of imagination, to great poets, to men who are enraptured by the felicitous expression of sentiment, and transported by an exquisite fancy or by the charms of nature, of truth, or of virtue! By their enthusiasm, by what they will tell you they have experienced, you will judge the cause by its effects; by that harmony which Borelli, a mere anatomist, understood better than all the Leibnizians, you will comprehend the material unity of man. In short, if the nerve-tension which causes pain occasions also the fever by which the distracted mind loses its will-power, and if, conversely, the mind too much excited, disturbs the body . . .; if an agitation rouses my desire and my ardent wish for what, a moment ago, I cared nothing about, and if in their turn certain brain impressions excite the same longing and the same desires, then why should we regard as double what is manifestly one being? In vain you fall back on the power of the will, since for one order that the will gives, it bows a hundred times to the yoke. And what wonder that in health the body obeys, since a torrent of blood and of animal spirits forces its obedience, and since the will has as ministers an invisible legion of fluids swifter than lightning and ever ready to do its bidding! But as the power of the will is exercised by means of the nerves, it is likewise limited by them.

Does the result of jaundice surprise you? Do you not know that the color of bodies depends on the color of the glasses through which we look at them, and that whatever is the color of the humors, such is the color of objects, at least, for us, vain playthings of a thousand illusions? But remove this color from the aqueous humor of the eye, let the bile flow through its natural filter, then the soul having new eyes, will no longer see yellow. Again, is it not thus, by removing cataract, or by injecting the Eustachian canal, that sight is restored to the blind, or hearing to the deaf? How many people, who were perhaps only clever charlatans, passed for miracle workers in the dark ages! Beautiful the soul, and powerful the will which can not act save by permission of the bodily conditions, and whose tastes change with age and fever! Should we, then, be astonished that philosophers have always had in mind the health of the body, to preserve the health of the soul, that Pythagoras gave rules for the diet as carefully as Plato forbade wine? The regime suited to the body is always the one with which sane physicians think they must begin, when it is a question of forming the mind, and of instructing it in the knowledge of truth and virtue; but these are vain words in the disorder of illness, and in the tumult of the senses. Without the precepts of hygiene. Epictetus, Socrates, Plato, and the rest preach in vain: all ethics is fruitless for one who lacks his share of temperance;

it is the source of all virtues as intemperance is the source
of all vices.

. . .

Grant only that organized matter is endowed with a principle of motion, which alone differentiates it from the inorganic . . . and that among animals, as I have sufficiently
proved, everything depends upon the diversity of this organization: these admissions suffice for guessing the riddle of
substances and of man. It [thus] appears that there is but
one [type of organization] in the universe, and that man is
the most perfect [example]. He is to the ape, and to the most
intelligent animals, as the planetary pendulum of Huyghens
is to a watch of Julien Leroy. More instruments, more wheels
and more springs were necessary to mark the movements of
the planets than to mark or strike the hours. . . . In like
fashion, it was necessary that nature should use more elabo-
rate art in making and sustaining a machine which for a
whole century could mark all motions of the heart and of the
mind: for though one does not tell time by the pulse, it is
at least the barometer of the warmth and the vivacity by
which one may estimate the nature of the soul. I am right!
The human body is a watch, a large watch constructed with
such skill and ingenuity, that if the wheel which marks the
seconds happens to stop, the minute wheel turns and keeps
on going its round, and in the same way the quarter-hour
wheel, and all the others go on running when the first wheels
have stopped because rusty or, for any reason, out of order.
. . . And is not this the reason why the loss of sight (caused
by the compression of the optic nerve and by its ceasing
to convey the images of objects) no more hinders hearing,
than the loss of hearing (caused by obstruction of the func-

tions of the auditory nerve) implies the loss of sight? In the same way, finally, does not one man hear . . . without being able to say that he hears, while another who hears nothing, but whose lingual nerves are uninjured in the brain, mechanically tells of all the dreams which pass through his mind? These phenomena do not surprise enlightened physicians at all. They know what to think about man's nature, and . . . of two physicians, the better one and the one who deserves more confidence is always, in my opinion, the one who is more versed in the physique or mechanism of the human body, and who, leaving aside the soul and all the anxieties which this chimera gives to fools and to ignorant men, is seriously occupied only in pure naturalism.

Therefore let the pretended M. Charp deride philosophers who have regarded animals as machines. How different is my view! I believe that Descartes would be a man in every way worthy of respect, if, born in a century that he had not been obliged to enlighten, he had known the value of experiment and observation, and the danger of cutting loose from them. But it is none the less just for me to make an authentic reparation to this great man for all the insignificant philosophers—poor jesters, and poor imitators of Locke—who instead of laughing impudently at Descartes, might better realize that without him the field of philosophy, like the field of science without Newton, might perhaps be still uncultivated.

This celebrated philosopher, it is true, was much deceived, and no one denies that. But at any rate he understood animal nature, he was the first to prove completely that animals are pure machines. And after a discovery of this importance demanding so much sagacity, how can we without ingratitude fail to pardon all his errors!

In my eyes, they are all atoned for by that great confession. For after all, although he extols the distinctness of the two substances, this is plainly but a trick of skill, a ruse of style, to make theologians swallow a poison, hidden in the shade of an analogy which strikes everybody else and which they alone fail to notice. For it is this, this strong analogy, which forces all scholars and wise judges to confess that these proud and vain beings, more distinguished by their pride than by the name of men however much they may wish to exalt themselves, are at bottom only animals and machines which, though upright, go on all fours. They all have this marvelous instinct, which is developed by education into mind, and which always has its seat in the brain, (or for want of that when it is lacking or hardened, in the medula oblongata) and never in the cerebellum; for I have often seen the cerebellum injured, and other observers have found it hardened, when the soul has not ceased to fulfil its functions.

To be a machine, to feel, to think, to know how to distinguish good from bad, as well as blue from yellow, in a word, to be born with an intelligence and a sure moral instinct, and to be but an animal, are therefore characters which are no more contradictory, than to be an ape or a parrot and to be able to give oneself pleasure . . . I believe that thought is so little incompatible with organized matter, that it seems to be one of its properties on a par with electricity, the faculty of motion, impenetrability, extension, etc.

Gustav Fechner (1801–1887)

Elements of Psychophysics

One of the most versatile, and volatile, personalities in the history of psychology—comparable to William James or Sigmund Freud in the vast range of his interests and productive achievement—Fechner began his long career as a physicist, was retired for several years as the result of a breakdown (partly induced by staring into the sun in order to obtain afterimages of it), spent fifteen years in the field of aesthetics, wrote laboriously metaphysical tracts demonstrating that plants have souls and that the physical world is animated, carried on a second career as a satirist under the pen name of "Dr. Mises," and almost incidentally performed the epoch-making experiments in psychophysics which were to give him enduring fame as the father of modern experimental psychology.

The great contribution of Fechner's *Elemente der Psychophysik*, published in 1860, was his development of a scale of measurement for the mind—relating sensation to stimulus in mathematical terms and hence giving promise that subjective mental events might be brought within the scope of objective science. But for all his rigorous psychophysicalism, Fechner did not seek to reduce mind to matter but believed fervently that body and mind were essentially identical and became separate only from two different viewpoints.

WEBER'S LAW, THAT EQUAL relative increments of stimuli are proportional to equal increments of sensation, is, in consideration of its generality and the wide limits within which it is absolutely or approximately valid, to be considered fundamental for psychic measurement. There are, however, limits to its validity as well as complications, which we shall have carefully to examine later. Yet even where this law ceases to be valid or absolute, the principle of psychic measurement continues to hold, inasmuch as any other relation between constant increments of sensation and variable increments of stimulus, even though it is arrived at empirically and expressed by an empirical formula, may serve equally well as the fundamental basis for psychic measurement, and indeed must serve as such in those parts of the stimulus scale where Weber's law loses its validity. In fact such a law, as well as Weber's law, will furnish a differential formula from which may be derived an integral formula containing an expression for the measurement of sensation.

This is a fundamental point of view, *in which Weber's law, with its limitations, appears, not as limiting the application of psychic measurement, but as restricted in its own application toward that end and beyond which application the general principle of psychic measurement nevertheless continues to hold.* It is not that the principle depends for its validity upon Weber's law, but merely that the application of the law is involved in the principle.

Accordingly investigation in the interest of the greatest possible generalization of psychic measurement has not essentially to commence with the greatest possible generalization of Weber's law, which might easily produce the questionable inclination to generalize the law beyond its natural limitation, or which might call forth the objection that the law was generalized beyond these limits solely in the interest of psychic measurement; but rather it may quite freely be asked how far Weber's law is applicable, and how far not; for the three methods which are used in psychic measurement are applicable even when Weber's law is not, and where these methods are applicable psychic measurement is possible.

In short, Weber's law forms merely the basis for the most numerous and important applications of psychic measurement, but not the universal and essential one. The most general and more fundamental basis for psychic measurement is rather those methods by which the relation between stimulus increments and sensation increment in general is determined, within, as well as without, the limits of Weber's law; and the development of these methods towards ever greater precision and perfection is the most important consideration in regard to psychic measurement.

And yet a great advantage would be lost, if so simple a law as Weber's law could not be used as an exact or at least sufficiently approximate basis for psychic measurement; just such an advantage as would be lost if we could not use the Kepler law in astronomy, or the laws of simple refraction in the theory of the dioptric instruments. Now there is just the same difficulty with these laws as with Weber's law. In the case of Kepler's law we abstract from deviations. In the case of simple lens refraction we abstract from optical aberration. In fact they may become invalid as soon as the simple hypotheses for which they are true no longer exist. Yet they will always remain decisive for the principle relation with which astronomy and dioptrics are concerned. Weber's law may in like manner, entirely lose its validity, as soon as the average or normal conditions under which the stimulus produces the sensation are unrealized. It will always, however, be decisive for these particular conditions.

Further, just as in physics and astronomy, so can we also in psychic measurement, neglect at first the irregularities and small departures from the law in order to discover and examine the principle relations with which the science has to do. The existence of these exceptions must not, however, be forgotten, inasmuch as the finer development and further progress of the science depends upon the determination and calculation of them, as soon as the possibility of doing so is given.

The determination of psychic measurement is a matter for outer psychophysics and its first applications lie within its boundary; its further applications and consequences, however, extend necessarily into the domain of inner psychophysics and its deeper meaning lies there. It must be remembered that the stimulus does not cause sensation directly, but rather through the assistance of bodily processes with which it stands in more direct connection. The dependence, quantitatively considered of sensation on stimulus, must finally be translated into one of sensation on the bodily processes which directly underlie the sensation—in short the psycho-physical processes; and the sensation, instead of being measured by the amount of the stimulus, will be measured by the intensity of these processes. In order to do this, the relation of the inner process to the stimulus must be known. Inasmuch as this is not a matter of direct experience it must be deduced by some exact method. Indeed it is possible for this entire investigation to proceed along exact lines, and it cannot fail at some time or other to obtain the success of a critical study, if one has not already reached that goal.

Although Weber's law, as applied to the relation of stimulus to sensation, shows only a limited validity in the domain of outer psychophysics, it has, as applied to the relation of sensation to kinetic energy, or as referred to some other function of the psycho-physical process, in all probability an unlimited validity in the domain of inner psychophysics, in that all exceptions to the law which we find in the arousal of sensation by external stimulus, are probably due to the fact that the stimulus only under normal or average conditions engenders a kinetic energy in those inner processes proportional to its own amount. From this it may be foreseen, that this law, after it has been restated as a relation between sensation and the psycho-physical processes, will be as important, general, and fundamental for the relations of mind to body, as is the law of gravity for the field of planetary motion. And it also has that simplicity which we are accustomed to find in fundamental laws of nature.

Although, then, physics measurement depends upon Weber's law only within certain limitations in the domain of outer psychophysics, it may well get its unconditional support from this law in the field of inner psychophysics. These are nevertheless for the present merely opinions and expectations, the verification of which lies in the future.

Wilhelm Wundt (1832–1920)

Principles of Physiological Psychology

"I am prepared to say that Wundt is the founder not of experimental psychology alone, but of psychology." So wrote the British-American psychologist, E. B. Titchener, shortly after the death of the most prolific and perhaps the most influential figure in the field of academic psychology. During his unusually long career—he died at the age of eighty-eight in the midst of new writings and revisions— Wundt virtually "founded" the discipline of psychology as an independent experimental science. In fact he inaugurated the first psychological laboratory, at the University of Leipzig in 1879, and there presided for half a century over the training of a host of future leaders both in Europe and America. During his sixty-eight productive years, according to one estimate, he produced 53,735 published pages of material—an output especially impressive in view of the enormous amount of technical research which preceded the writing. He contributed systematically to nearly every topic in psychology: sensation, feeling, perception, emotion, language, and so on. Moreover, he ranged far afield; his earliest work, after receiving an M.D. degree in 1856, was in physiology, in which he wrote a textbook and a manual of medical physics. Later, in his "philosophical decade" (the 1880's), Wundt composed separate volumes in logic, in ethics, and in philosophy as a system. His most famous and comprehensive work, of course, was in psychology— notably his *Physiologische Psychologie*, for two generations the standard work on physiological psychology, and the

Volkerpsychologie (Collective Psychology), a massive ten-volume compendium of psychological and philosophical knowledge which required nearly twenty years to complete.

Wundt was, as E. G. Boring has observed, "an encyclo-pedist and a systematizer"; he also possessed the reflective temperament of a philosopher and the zeal of a polemicist. Although generally regarded as the father of experimental psychology, he did not claim that the experimental method was sufficient or appropriate for all psychological inquiry, and himself used the method for the most part to illustrate conclusions arrived at by more speculative means. Follow-ing the associationist tradition, Wundt reduced mind and consciousness into elements (his system has been called a "mental chemistry"), which themselves have attributes and are connected by associations. In his middle years Wundt developed a "three-dimensional" theory of feeling, which made it possible to distinguish six principal qualities of feeling, organized in three pairs of opposites: i.e., pleasure-unpleasure, strain-relaxation, excitement-calm. The publi-cation of this theory led to a generation of excited effort in the laboratories of two continents as experimental psychol-ogists sought to confirm or refute the concept of the acknowledged master.

The present selection is taken from the work which (in the opinion of J. C. Flügel) "is often considered to be the most important book in the whole history of psychology," the *Grundzuge der Physiologischen Psychologie*, which went through several editions following its publication in 1873–74 and became in effect the bible for successive generations of students.

THE PROBLEM OF PHYSIOLOGICAL PSYCHOLOGY

THE TITLE OF THE present work is in itself a sufficiently clear indication of the contents. In it, the attempt is made to show the connexion between two sciences whose subject-matters are closely interrelated, but which have, for the most part, followed wholly divergent paths. Physiology and psychology cover, between them, the field of vital phenomena; they deal with the facts of life at large, and in particular with the facts of human life. Physiology is concerned with all those phenomena of life that present themselves to us in sense perception as bodily processes, and accordingly, form part of that total environment which we name the external world. Psychology, on the other hand, seeks to give account of the interconnexion of processes which are evinced by our own consciousness, or which we infer from such manifestations of the bodily life in other creatures as indicate the presence of a consciousness similar to our own.

This division of vital processes into physical and psychical is useful and even necessary for the solution of scientific problems. We must, however, remember that the life of an organism is really one; complex, it is true, but still unitary. We can, therefore, no more separate the processes of bodily life from conscious processes than we can mark off an outer experience, mediated by sense perceptions, and oppose it, as something wholly separate and apart, to what we call "inner" experience, the events of our own consciousness. On the contrary: just as one and the same thing, e.g., a tree that I perceive before me, falls as external object within the scope of natural science, and as conscious contents within that of psychology, so there are many phenomena of the physical life that are uniformly connected with conscious processes, while these in turn are always bound up with processes in the living body. It is a matter of every-day experience that we refer certain bodily movements directly to volitions, which we can observe as such only in our consciousness. Conversely, we refer the ideas of external objects that arise in consciousness either to direct affection of the organs of sense, or, in the case of memory images, to physiological excitations within the sensory centres, which we interpret as after-effects of foregone sense impressions.

It follows then, that physiology and psychology have many points of contact. In general, there can of course be no doubt that their problems are distinct. But psychology is called upon to trace out the relations that obtain between conscious processes and certain phenomena of the physical life; and physiology, on its side, cannot afford to neglect the conscious contents in which certain phenomena of this bodily life manifest themselves to us. Indeed, as regards physiology, the interdependence of the two sciences is plainly in evidence. Practically everything that the physiologists tell us, by way of fact or of hypothesis, concerning the processes in the organs of sense and in the brain, is based upon determinate mental symptoms: so that psychology has long been recognised, explicitly or implicitly, as an indispensable auxiliary of physiological investigation. Psychologists, it is true, have been apt to take a different attitude towards physiology. They have tended to regard as superfluous any reference to the physical organism; they have supposed that nothing more is required for a science of mind than the direct apprehension of conscious processes themselves. It is in token of dissent from any such standpoint that the present work is entitled a "physiological psychology." We take issue, upon this matter, with every treatment of psychology that is based on simple self-observation or on philosophical presuppositions. We shall, whenever the occasion seems to demand, employ physiology in the service of psychology. We are thus, as was indicated above, following the example of physiology itself, which has never been in a position to disregard facts that properly belong to psychology,—although it has often been hampered in its use of them by the defects of the empirical or metaphysical psychology which it has found current.

Physiological psychology is, therefore, first of all *psychology*. It has in view the same principal object upon which all other forms of psychological exposition are directed: *the investigation of conscious processes in the modes of connexion peculiar to them*. It is not a province of physiology; nor does it attempt, as has been mistakenly asserted, to derive or explain the phenomena of the psychical from those of the physical life. We may read this meaning into the phrase "physiological psychology," just as we might interpret the title "microscopical anatomy" to mean a discussion, with illustrations from anatomy, of what has been accomplished by the microscope; but the words should be no more misleading in the one case than they are in the other. As employed in the present work, the adjective "physiological" implies simply that our psychology will avail itself to the full of the means that modern physiology puts at its disposal for the analysis of conscious processes. It will do this in two ways.

(1) Psychological inquiries have, up to the most recent times, been undertaken solely in the interest of philosophy; physiology was enabled, by the character of its problems, to advance more quickly towards the application of exact experimental methods. Since, however, the experimental modification of the processes of life, as practised by physiology, oftentimes effects a concomitant change, direct or indirect, in the processes of consciousness,—which, as we have seen, form part of vital processes at large,—it is clear that physiology is, in the very nature of the case, qualified to assist psychology on the side of *method*; thus rendering the same help to psychology that it itself received from physics. In so far as physiological psychology receives assistance from physiology in the elaboration of experimental methods, it may be termed *experimental psychology*. This name suggests, what should not be forgotten, that psychology, in adopting the experi-

mental methods of physiology, does not by any means take them over as they are, and apply them without change to a new material. The methods of experimental psychology have been transformed—in some instances, actually remodelled —by psychology itself, to meet the specific requirements of psychological investigation. Psychology has adapted physiological, as physiology adapted psychical methods, to its own ends.

(2) An adequate definition of life, taken in the wider sense, must (as we said just now) cover both the vital processes of the physical organism and the processes of consciousness. Hence, wherever we meet with vital phenomena that present the two aspects, physical and psychical, there naturally arises a question as to the relations in which these aspects stand to each other. So we come face to face with a whole series of special problems, which may be occasionally touched upon by physiology or psychology, but which cannot receive their final solution at the hands of either, just by reason of that division of labour to which both sciences alike stand committed. Experimental psychology is no better able to cope with them than is any other form of psychology, seeing that it differs from its rivals only in method, and not in aim or purpose. Physiological psychology, on the other hand, is competent to investigate the relations that hold between the processes of the physical and those of the mental life. And in so far as it accepts this second problem, we may name it a *psychophysics*. If we free this term from any sort of metaphysical implication as to the relation of mind and body, and understand by it nothing more than an investigation of the relations that may be shown empirically to obtain between the psychical and the physical aspects of vital processes, it is clear at once that psychophysics becomes for us not, what it is sometimes taken to be, a science intermediate between

physiology and psychology, but rather a science that is auxiliary to both. It must, however, render service more especially to psychology, since the relations existing between determinate conditions of the physical organisation, on the one hand, and the processes of consciousness, on the other, are primarily of interest to the psychologist. In its final purpose, therefore, this psychophysical problem that we have assigned to physiological psychology proves to be itself psychological. In execution, it will be predominantly physiological, since psychophysics is concerned to follow up the anatomical and physiological investigation of the bodily substrates of conscious processes, and to subject its results to critical examination with a view to their bearing upon our psychical life.

There are thus two problems which are suggested by the title "physiological psychology": the problem of *method*, which involves the application of experiment, and the problem of a psychophysical *supplement*, which involves a knowledge of the bodily substrates of the mental life. For psychology itself, the former is the more essential; the second is of importance mainly for the philosophical question of the unitariness of vital processes at large. As an experimental science, physiological psychology seeks to accomplish a reform in psychological investigation comparable with the revolution brought about in the natural sciences by the introduction of the experimental method. From one point of view, indeed, the change wrought is still more radical: for while in natural science it is possible, under favorable conditions, to make an accurate observation without recourse to experiment, there is no such possibility in psychology. It is only with grave reservations that what is called "pure self-observation" can properly be termed observation at all, and under no circumstances can it lay claim to accuracy. On the other hand, it is of the essence of experiment that we can vary the conditions of an occurrence at will and, if we are aiming at exact results, in a quantitatively determinable way. Hence, even in the domain of natural science, the aid of the experimental method becomes indispensable whenever the problem set is the analysis of transient and impermanent phenomena, and not merely the observation of persistent and relatively constant objects. But conscious contents are at the opposite pole from permanent objects; they are processes, fleeting occurrences, in continual flux and change. In their case, therefore, the experimental method is of cardinal importance; it and it alone makes a scientific introspection possible. For all accurate observation implies that the object of observation (in this case the psychical process) can be held fast by the attention, and any changes that it undergoes attentively followed. And this fixation by the attention implies, in its turn, that the observed object is independent of the observer. Now it is obvious that the required independence does not obtain in any attempt at a direct self-observation, undertaken without the help of experiment. The endeavour to observe oneself must inevitably introduce changes into the course of mental events,—changes which could not have occurred without it, and whose usual consequence is that the very process which was to have been observed disappears from consciousness. The psychological experiment proceeds very differently. In the first place, it creates external conditions that look towards the production of a determinate mental process at a given moment. In the second place, it makes the observer so far master of the general situation, that the state of consciousness accompanying this process remains approximately unchanged. The great importance of the experimental method, therefore, lies not simply in the fact that, here as in the physical realm, it enables us arbitrarily to vary the conditions of our observations, but also and essentially in the further fact that it makes observation itself possible for us. The results of this observation may then be fruitfully employed in the examination of other mental phenomena, whose nature prevents their own direct experimental modification.

We may add that, fortunately for the science, there are other sources of objective psychological knowledge, which become accessible at the very point where the experimental method fails us. These are certain products of the common mental life, in which we may trace the operation of determinate psychical motives: chief among them are language, myth and custom. In part determined by historical conditions, they are also, in part, dependent upon universal psychological laws; and the phenomena that are referable to these laws form the subject-matter of a special psychological discipline, *ethnic* psychology. The results of ethnic psychology constitute, at the same time, our chief source of information regarding the general psychology of the complex mental processes. In this way, experimental psychology and ethnic psychology form the two principal departments of scientific psychology at large. They are supplemented by *child* and *animal* psychology, which in conjunction with ethnic psychology attempt to resolve the problems of psychogenesis. Workers in both these fields may, of course, avail themselves within certain limits of the advantages of the experimental method. But the results of experiment are here matters of objective observation only, and the experimental method accordingly loses the peculiar significance which it possesses as an instrument of introspection. Finally, child psychology and experimental psychology in the narrower sense may be bracketed together as *individual* psychology, while animal psychology and ethnic psychology form the two halves of a *generic* or *comparative* psychology. These distinctions within psychology are, however, by no means to be put on a level with the analogous divisions of the province of physiology. Child psychology and animal psychology are of relatively slight importance, as compared with the sciences which deal with the corresponding physiological problems of ontogeny and phylogeny. On the other hand, ethnic psychology must always come to the assistance of individual psychology, when the developmental forms of the complex mental processes are in question.

Ivan Pavlov (1849–1936)

On Conditioned Reflexes

The discovery by Pavlov in 1902 of the phenomenon which he called the "conditioned reflex" struck many experimental psychologists, particularly in America, with the force of a revelation. In principle the discovery represented only new laboratory evidence for an old theory—the law of association by contiguity in time—but in practice it was heralded as the key to the comprehension and control of the whole range of human behavior. Pavlov's reflexology was an elaboration of the famous experiments with the salivary reflex in dogs; its essential point is that a response which ordinarily results from a given stimulus will result from another and different stimulus if the latter is frequently presented just prior to the former; thus the association of a bell with the presentation of food will lead to the new or "conditioned response" upon the presentation of the bell alone. This process of conditioning is, as Boring has noted, "an objective substitute for introspection," a means of determining the perceptions and discriminations of an animal which cannot directly communicate such data to the human experimenter.

The apparent success of Pavlov and his fellow reflexologists (notably his colleague V. M. Bekhterev) led such psychologists as John B. Watson to herald the birth of a new era of scientific psychology which would make possible not only the perfect understanding of human conduct but its deliberate transformation as well. The manipulative propensities of conditioned reflexology, which in America were at first thought to shadow forth a truly democratic psychology, were not lost upon the Soviet government following the Russian Revolution of 1917. Reflexology became the official psychology of the Soviet Union, with Pavlov installed as its high priest (although he himself was no dogmatist nor even a materialist); and until recently, virtually all deviations (such as Freudian psychoanalysis) from this thoroughly physiological psychology were banished from the U.S.S.R. as dangerous heresy.

First of all, I consider it my duty to thank the Philosophical Society for expressing readiness, through its chairman, to listen to what I have to say. I do not know to what extent my subject will be of interest to the members. As for myself, however, I have a special purpose which will be revealed at the end of my address.

I wish to inform you of the results of very extensive research carried out by me in the course of many years jointly with a dozen or so colleagues who constantly participated in it both with their heads and with their hands. Without their co-operation, this work would have been only one-tenth of what it is. So that when I use the word "I," you should take it not in the narrow sense of an author, but, so to speak, in the sense of a conductor. In the main I guided and co-ordinated the work.

Now for the essence of my subject.

Let us take any higher animal, for example, the dog. Although it is not at the top of the zoological ladder (the monkey occupies a higher place), it is closer to man than any other animal and has been his companion since prehistoric times. I heard the late zoologist Modest Bogdanov state the following when reviewing prehistoric man and his companions, especially the dog: "Justice compels us to say that it is the dog that helped man to become what he is." Such is his appreciation of the dog. Consequently, the dog is not just an ordinary animal. Indeed, consider a watch-dog, a hunter, a domestic pet, etc.; before your eyes is their entire activity in all its higher manifestations, or, as the Americans are inclined to call it, their entire behaviour. If I wished to study this higher activity of the dog, that is, to systematize the phenomena of its life and to disclose the laws and rules which govern them, the following question would inevitably confront me: how shall I act and which way shall I choose? Generally speaking, there are two ways. One is the ordinary way taken by everybody. It consists in attributing the human inner world to the animal, that is, in assuming that the animal thinks, feels, desires, etc., in much the same way as we do. Consequently, this means guessing what takes place within the animal and interpreting its behaviour on the basis of these suppositions. The other way is entirely different; this is the way of natural science which considers the phenomena, the facts, from a purely external aspect, and which in the given case would concentrate only on the agents of the external world that act on the dog, as well as on the visible reactions of the dog to these agents.

The question, therefore, is this: which way is preferable, more expedient, the best way to tackle the problem? Allow me to answer this question, which is of great importance, by presenting the facts in chronological order. Several decades ago my laboratory made a study of the digestive process, and specially investigated the activity of the digestive glands producing the digestive juices by means of which the food is transformed, assimilated by the organism and enters into the vital chemical processes. Our job was to study all the conditions which determined the work of these glands. Much of our investigation was devoted to the first of these glands, the salivary gland. A detailed and systematic study of the latter demonstrated that its work is extremely delicate and highly adaptable to whatever substance enters the mouth, and that the quantity and quality of saliva show corresponding considerable fluctuations. When the ingested food is dry, there is an abundant secretion of saliva, since the food must be moistened; when the food is moist, the amount of saliva is smaller. If it is a matter of food which must pass into the stomach, the saliva is rich in mucus; it lubricates the mass of food and thereby facilitates its ingestion. But when there is a substance which must be ejected from the mouth, the saliva is watery and helps to rinse the mouth.

Thus, we see a series of delicate co-ordinations between the work of the salivary gland and the kind of substance upon which the saliva is secreted. Next comes the question: what underlies this delicate co-ordination, what is its mechanism? The physiologist—and that is my specialty—has a ready answer to this question. The properties of the food act on the nerve endings and stimulate them. These nervous impulses proceed to definite points of the central nervous system and thence to the nerves leading to the salivary gland. In this way there arises an obvious connection between the substance which enters the mouth and the work of the gland. The particulars of this connection are explained by the fact that the nerves from the oral cavity, where the substances act, are separately excited by acid, sweet, rough, soft, hard, hot, cold, etc.; thus the impulses are conducted now by one nerve, now by another. In the central nervous system these impulses are transmitted to the salivary gland along different nerves. Some of them evoke one kind of activity, the others—activity of a different kind. Consequently, the different properties of the food stimulate different nerves, and in the central nervous system there takes place a transfer of the impulses to corresponding nerves which evoke one or another activity.

Since we aimed at a complete investigation we had to consider all the concomitant conditions, apart from those I have just mentioned. The substances introduced into the mouth act on the salivary gland. But does the same thing occur when food is placed in front of the dog, i.e., is it effective at a distance? We know very well that when we are hungry, the sight of food evokes in us a flow of saliva. Hence, the expression "the mouth waters." It was, therefore, necessary to investigate this phenomena as well. What does it mean, especially since in this case there is no contact with food substances at all? Concerning these facts physiology used to say that in addition to ordinary stimulation, there is psychical stimulation of the salivary gland. Very well. But what does this imply, how is it to be interpreted, how must we, physiologists, tackle the question? We could not ignore it, because it played a certain part. On what grounds could we discard it?

Let us, first of all, consider the bare fact of psychical excitation. It turned out that psychical excitation, i.e., the action of a substance at a distance, is exactly the same as when it is in the mouth. It is absolutely the same in all respects. Depending on the kind of food shown to the dog, whether dry or liquid, edible or absolutely inedible, the salivary gland functions in exactly the same way as when these substances are introduced into the mouth. The psychical excitation reveals exactly the same relations, but on a somewhat smaller scale. How, then, is this to be studied? Naturally, when we see a dog eat rapidly, snatch the food and chew it for a long time, we think, willy-nilly, that the animal strongly desires to eat, and that it is this that makes it rush to the food and swallow it. It longs to eat. Another time the

dog's movements are slow and languid, and so we say that it
has no great desire to eat. When it eats, you see the work
of the muscles alone, which is fully aimed at introducing the
food into the mouth, at chewing and swallowing it. Judging
by all this, one would say that the dog experiences pleasure
in eating. On the contrary, when an inedible substance gets
into the mouth, and the dog ejects it, forces it out with the
help of the tongue and by shaking its head, we involuntarily
say that this is unpleasant for the animal.

Now, when we decided to elucidate and analyse this phenomenon, we at first adopted this trite point of view. We took
into account the feelings, desires, imagination, etc., of our
animal. And this resulted in a quite unexpected and extraordinary fact: one of my colleagues and I irreconcilably
differed in opinion. We could not come to agreement, could
not convince each other as to who was right; for decades
prior to this, as well as afterwards, we always reached agreement on all questions, one way or another, but the given case
ended in complete discord. This made us meditate on the
matter. It seemed probable that we were not on the right
track. And the more we thought about the matter, the more
convinced we became that another course of investigation
should be followed. Overcoming the difficulties which I experienced in the beginning, and taking the way of persistent
thought and concentrated attention, I finally reached the
ground of true objectivity. Such psychological expressions,
as the dog guessed, wished, desired, etc., were wholly withdrawn from our use (in our laboratory a fine was even imposed on their use).

Finally, all the phenomena with which we were concerned
appeared to us in a new light. So what, then, is the point?
What is that which the physiologists term psychical stimulation of the salivary gland? We naturally, put ourselves the

question: is it not a form of nervous activity, long ago established by physiology and well known to physiologists? Is it not a reflex? And what does this reflex of the physiologist represent?

It consists of three chief elements. In the first place, there is an indispensable external agent producing the stimulation. In the second place, there is a definite nervous path by means of which the external impulse makes itself felt in the effector organ. This is the so-called reflex arc, a chain composed of an afferent nerve, a central part and a centrifugal or efferent nerve. And finally, in the third place, the law-governed, but not accidental or capricious, nature of the reaction. Given certain conditions the reaction always and invariably arises. Of course, this must not be understood in the sense of absolute constancy, in other words, as meaning that circumstances may never occur in which the agent does not act. It is obvious that there can be conditions in which the action remains disguised. According to the law of gravity all things must fall to the earth, but once you support them this does not occur.

Now let us return to our subject. What, then, is the psychical stimulation of the salivary gland? When food is placed in front of the animal, before its eyes, it certainly acts on the animal, on its eye, ear, nose. No essential difference between this action and that in the mouth is observed. There are reflexes from the eye and from the ear. Upon hearing a loud sound we start—a reflex action. Under the action of a strong light the pupils of our eyes contract. Hence, this does not interfere with our concept that what we call psychical stimulation is a reflex. The second element, the nervous path, is, obviously, also present here; for when the dog sees the food, the nervous path originates not from the nerves of the mouth, but from those of the eye, then proceeds to the central nervous system and from there puts the salivary gland into action. Again there is no essential difference here, and there is nothing to prevent us from representing this as a reflex. Let us now examine the third element— the law-governed nature of the reaction. In this respect the following must be pointed out: the given stimulation acts less regularly, less often than when the stimulant is in the mouth. However, it is possible to acquire such a degree of knowledge and mastery of the subject that all the conditions on which the action of the substance at a distance depends will be under our control. If this has been attained (which is now the case), then the law-governed nature of the reaction is in evidence.

But the "psychical" excitation has an additional feature. When we examine these phenomena more closely, it appears that among the agents acting at a distance there may be some which did not exist previously. Here is an example. Let us suppose that the attendant enters for the first time the chamber in which the dog is kept and brings in the food. The food begins to act the moment it is shown to the dog. And if the same attendant brings in the food several days in succession the upshot will be that the moment he opens the door and puts his head in, the action begins. Thus, a new stimulating agent has appeared. If this is continued long enough, then the sound of the attendant's steps alone is sufficient to evoke a secretion of saliva. Consequently, stimuli that did not exist before have now developed. The difference appears to be considerable and essential: while in the physiological stimulation the stimuli are constant, here they are variable. However, this point can be interpreted in the following way: should the new stimulus become effective under strictly definite conditions, which also can be determined by the experimenter, i.e., if the entire phenomenon obeys certain laws as well, then this cannot serve as an objection. Although the stimuli are new, they inevitably arise under definite conditions. Accident is ruled out. Here, too, the phenomena are related to definite laws. I can say that just as the first reflex was characterized by the presence of a stimulus which travelled along a definite path and, in certain circumstances, evoked our phenomenon, here, too, the phenomenon arises under strictly definite conditions. The essence, the composition of the concept of reflex has not changed in the least.

It has been proved that any agent of the external world can be made a stimulus of the salivary gland. Any sound, odour, etc., may become a stimulus that will excite the salivary gland exactly in the same way as it is excited by food at a distance. As to the precision of the fact, there is no difference whatever; it is only necessary to take into account the conditions in which the fact exists. What, then, are the conditions which can become stimuli of the salivary gland? The chief condition is coincidence in time. The experiment is performed as follows. We take, for example, a certain sound which has no relation to the salivary gland. This sound acts on the dog. Then we feed the dog or introduce acid into its mouth. After several repetitions of this the sound itself, without the addition of food or acid, begins to excite the salivary gland. There are altogether four or five, at most six conditions under which any stimulant, any agent of the external world, becomes a stimulus of the salivary gland in the dog. Once this is so, once it has become a stimulus under a definite series of conditions, it will always act with the same precision as food or as any rejected substance introduced into the mouth. If any external agent invariably becomes a stimulus of the salivary gland under definite conditions, and having become such, inevitably produces its action, then what grounds are there for saying that in essence this is anything other than a reflex? Actually this is a law-governed reaction of the organism to an external agent effected through the medium of a definite part of the nervous system.

As I have said, the ordinary reflex is formed like this: there is a definite nervous path along which the stimulation proceeding from the peripheral part is conducted to the effector organ, in the given case, the salivary gland. This conducting path is, so to speak, a live wire. But what happens in this case? Here it should be added that the nervous system is not only a conducting apparatus, as is generally regarded, but also a connecting one. And there is nothing paradoxical in this supposition. If in everyday life we widely use contactors, for example, in electric lighting, telephone communication, etc., then it would be strange indeed if in the most perfect machine on earth, there were no application of the principle of connection, but only of conduction. Hence, it is quite natural that along with conducting properties the nervous system should also possess a connecting apparatus. Analysis has shown that the constant form of stimulation of the salivary gland by food at a distance, which is an ordinary case known to everybody, is a similar formation of a new nervous path by means of connection.

While working in Prof. Vartanov's laboratory, Dr. I. S. Tsitovich performed the following interesting experiment. He took a new-born puppy and fed it exclusively on milk for several months; the puppy had known no other food. Then he subjected it to an operation so that the work of the salivary gland could be observed; afterwards he showed the puppy foods other than milk. But not one of them, shown at a distance, produced any effect on the salivary gland. Consequently, when different foods act from a distance, this is a reflex newly formed as a result of individual life experience. The matter can be described thus: when a piece of meat is first placed before a puppy several months old neither its appearance nor its odour produce any action on the salivary gland. It is necessary that the food be taken into the puppy's mouth at least once, to evoke a simple, purely conducting reflex, and only then there develops a new reflex to the appearance and odour of the meat. And so, gentlemen, you see that we have to recognize the existence of two kinds of reflexes: one is ready from the time of birth, and is of a purely conducting character, and the other is continuously, incessantly being formed in the course of individual life, obeys exactly the same laws, but rests on the basis of another property of our nervous system—on connection.

The first reflex can be termed inborn, and the other—acquired, or respectively—generic and individual. The inborn, generic, constant and stereotyped reflex we termed unconditioned; the other, which depends on a multitude of conditions and constantly fluctuates in conformity with the circumstances, we called conditioned; in this way we characterized the reflexes from the standpoint of practice, from the point of view of laboratory investigation. The conditioned reflex is also indispensable, and thus, like the unconditioned reflex, belongs entirely to the domain of physiology. With this formulation physiology, of course, comes into possession of an enormous mass of new material, since there is an infinite number of these conditioned reflexes. Our life consists of a multitude of inborn reflexes. When one says that there are three kinds of these reflexes, namely, the self-defensive, the alimentary and the sexual, this is undoubtedly only an academic scheme; actually, they are numerous, and they must be divided and subdivided. Consequently, there is a multitude even of these simple, inborn reflexes; as for conditioned reflexes their number is endless.

John B. Watson (1878–1958)

What Is Behaviorism?

"The cry of the behaviorist," announced John B. Watson, "is 'Give me the baby and my world to bring it up in and I'll make it crawl and walk; I'll make it climb and use its hands in constructing buildings of stone or wood; I'll make it a thief, a gunman, or a dope fiend. The possibility of shaping in any direction is almost endless.' "* With this bravura style, Watson in the second decade of the present century ushered in an aggressive movement which swept the psychological laboratories of the nation and was all but universally regarded as a revolution in the name of Science and Democracy. "For a while in the 1920's," as one historian recalls, "it seemed as if all America had gone behaviorist. Everyone (except the few associated with Titchener) was a behaviorist and no behaviorist agreed with any other."† The sense of revelation, not to say of salvation, felt by many upon the advent of Watsonian behaviorism was expressed by a reviewer of one of his books: "Perhaps this is the most important book ever written. One stands for an instant blinded with a great hope."

The main tenets of the behaviorist's creed are plainly set forth in the selection that follows, and need not be

---

*John B. Watson, *The Ways of Behaviorism* (New York: Harper, 1926), pp. 9, 35.

†Edwin G. Boring, *A History of Experimental Psychology*, Second Edition (New York: Appleton-Century-Crofts, 1950), p. 645.

duplicated here. But it should be noted that Watson's rigorously mechanistic S-R psychology, with its insistent repudiation of mind and purpose as "medieval conceptions," stripped the human person of any capacity for rationality or responsibility and left him as the helpless puppet of whatever forces may play upon him. Behaviorism in Watson's hands was no merely descriptive science; it sought to shape the baby and the adult alike in the direction of conformity and good behavior. "The interest of the behaviorist is more than the interest of a spectator," declared Watson; "he wants to control man's reactions as physical scientists want to control and manipulate other natural phenomena.* It is amusing in a rather absurdist way to recall that Watson himself moved quickly from the academy, following his first popular success, into the vice-presidency of an advertising agency. By the mid-1930's the behaviorist movement had lost its radical force and insurgent appeal, and had given way to newer fashions in psychology; but it would be a mistake to suppose that its basic claims and assumptions were no longer adhered to. One year before Watson's death, the American Psychological Association presented him with an official citation which read: "To Dr. John B. Watson, whose work has been one of the vital determinants of the form and substance of modern psychology. He initiated a revolution in psychological thought, and his writings have been the point of departure for continuing lines of fruitful research."†

The following selection is taken from Watson's *Behaviorism*.

TWO OPPOSED POINTS OF view are still dominant in American psychological thinking—introspective or subjective psychology, and behaviorism or objective psychology.[1] Until the

---

*John B. Watson, *Behaviorism* (Chicago: University of Chicago Press, 1958 edition), p. 5. (This book was first published in 1924.)

†Quoted in Watson, *ibid.*, p. iii.

advent of behaviorism in 1912, introspective psychology completely dominated American university psychological life.

The conspicuous leaders of introspective psychology in the first decade of the twentieth century were E. B. Titchener of Cornell and William James of Harvard. The death of James in 1910 and the death of Titchener in 1927 left introspective psychology without emotional leadership. Although Titchener's psychology differed in many points from that of William James, their fundamental assumptions were the same. In the first place, both were of German origin. In the second place, and of more importance, both claimed that *consciousness is the subject matter of psychology*.

Behaviorism, on the contrary, holds that the subject matter of human psychology *is the behavior of the human being*. Behaviorism claims that consciousness is neither a definite nor a usable concept. The behaviorist, who has been trained always as an experimentalist, holds, further, that belief in the existence of consciousness goes back to the ancient days of superstition and magic.

The great mass of the people even today has not yet progressed very far away from savagery—it wants to believe in magic. The savage believes that incantations can bring rain, good crops, good hunting, that an unfriendly voodoo doctor can bring disaster to a person or to a whole tribe; that an enemy who has obtained a nail paring or a lock of your hair can cast a harmful spell over you and control your actions. There is always interest and news in magic. Almost every era has its new magic, black or white, and its new magician. Moses had his magic: he smote the rock and water gushed out. Christ had his magic: he turned water into wine and raised the dead to life. Coué had his magic word formula. Mrs. Eddy had a similar one.

Magic lives forever. As time goes on, all of these critically undigested, innumerably told tales get woven into the folk lore of the people. Folk lore in turn gets organized into religions. Religions get caught up into the political and economic network of the country. Then they are used as tools. The public is forced to accept all of the old wives' tales, and it passes them on as gospel to its children's children.

The extent to which most of us are shot through with a savage background is almost unbelievable. Few of us escape it. Not even a college education seems to correct it. If anything, it seems to strengthen it, since the colleges themselves are filled with instructors who have the same background. Some of our greatest biologists, physicists, and chemists, when outside of their laboratories, fall back upon folk lore which has become crystallized into religious concepts. These concepts—these heritages of a timid savage past—have made the emergence and growth of scientific psychology extremely difficult.

AN EXAMPLE OF SUCH CONCEPTS

One example of such a religious concept is that every individual has a *soul* which is separate and distinct from the *body*. This soul is really a part of a supreme being. This ancient view led to the philosophical platform called "dualism." This dogma has been present in human psychology from earliest antiquity. No one has ever touched a soul, or seen one in a test tube, or has in any way come into relationship with it as he has with the other objects of his daily experience. Nevertheless, to doubt its existence is to become a heretic and once might possibly even have led to the loss of one's head. Even today the man holding a public position dare not question it.

With the development of the physical sciences which came with the renaissance, a certain release from this stifling soul cloud was obtained. A man could think of astronomy, of the celestial bodies and their motions, of gravitation and the like, without involving soul. Although the early scientists were as a rule devout Christians, nevertheless they began to leave soul out of their test tubes.

Psychology and philosophy, however, in dealing as they thought with non-material objects, found it difficult to escape the language of the church, and hence the concept of mind or soul as distinct from the body came down almost unchanged in essence to the latter part of the nineteenth century.

Wundt, the real father of experimental psychology, unquestionably wanted in 1879 a scientific psychology. He grew up in the midst of a dualistic philosophy of the most pronounced type. He could not see his way clear to a solution of the mind-body problem. His psychology, which has reigned supreme to the present day, is necessarily a compromise. He substituted the term *consciousness* for the term soul. Consciousness is not quite so unobservable as soul. We observe it by peeking in suddenly and catching it unawares as it were *(introspection)*.

Wundt had an immense following. Just as now it is fashionable to go to Vienna to study psycho-analysis under Freud, just so was it fashionable some forty years ago to study at Leipzig with Wundt. The men who returned founded the laboratories at Johns Hopkins University, the University of Pennsylvania, Columbia, Clark and Cornell. All were equipped to do battle with the elusive (almost soul-like) thing called consciousness.

To show how unscientific is the main concept behind this great German-American school of psychology, look for a moment at William James' definition of psychology. "Psychology is the description and explanation of states of consciousness as such." Starting with a definition which *assumes* what he starts out to prove, he escapes his difficulty by an *argumentum ad hominem.* Consciousness—Oh, yes, everybody must know what this "consciousness" is. When we have a sensation of red, a perception, a thought, when we *will* to do something, or when we *purpose* to do something, or when we desire to do something, we are being *conscious.*

All other introspectionists are equally illogical. In other words, they do not tell us what consciousness is, but merely begin to put things into it by assumption; and then when they come to analyze consciousness, naturally they find in it just what they put into it. Consequently, in the analyses of consciousness made by certain of the psychologists you find such elements as *sensations* and their ghosts, the *images.* With others you find not only sensations, but so-called *affective elements*; in still others you find such elements as *will*—the so-called *conative element* in consciousness. With some psychologists you find many hundreds of sensations of a certain type; others maintain that only a few of that type exist. And so it goes. Literally hundreds of thousands of printed pages have been published on the minute analysis of this intangible something called "consciousness." And how do we begin work upon it? Not by analyzing it as we would a chemical compound, or the way a plant grows. No, those things are material things. This thing we call consciousness can be analyzed only by *introspection*—a looking in on what takes place inside of us.

As a result of this major assumption that there is such a thing as consciousness and that we can analyze it by introspection, we find as many analyses as there are individual psychologists. There is no way of experimentally attacking and solving psychological problems and standardizing methods.

THE ADVENT OF THE BEHAVIORISTS

In 1912 the objective psychologists or behaviorists reached the conclusion that they could no longer be content to work with Wundt's formulations. They felt that the thirty-odd barren years since the establishment of Wundt's laboratory had proved conclusively that the so-called introspective psychology of Germany was founded upon wrong hypotheses— that no psychology which included the religious mind-body problem could ever arrive at verifiable conclusions. They decided either to give up psychology or else to make it a natural science. They saw their brother-scientists making progress in medicine, in chemistry, in physics. Every new discovery in those fields was of prime importance; every new element isolated in one laboratory could be isolated in some other laboratory; each new element was immediately taken up in the warp and woof of science as a whole. One need only mention wireless, radium, insulin, thyroxin, to verify this. Elements so isolated and methods so formulated immediately began to function in human achievement.

In his first efforts to get uniformity in subject matter and in methods the behaviorist began his own formulation of the problem of psychology by sweeping aside all mediaeval conceptions. He dropped from his scientific vocabulary all subjective terms such as sensation, perception, image, desire, purpose, and even thinking and emotion as they were subjectively defined.

THE BEHAVIORIST'S PLATFORM

The behaviorist asks: Why don't we make what we can *observe* the real field of psychology? Let us limit ourselves to things that can be observed, and formulate laws concerning only those things. Now what can we observe? We can observe *behavior—what the organism does or says.* And let us point out at once: that *saying* is doing—that is, *behaving.* Speaking overtly or to ourselves (thinking) is just as objective a type of behavior as baseball.

The rule, or measuring rod, which the behaviorist puts in

front of him always is: Can I describe this bit of behavior I see in terms of "stimulus and response"? By stimulus we mean any object in the general environment or any change in the tissues themselves due to the physiological condition of the animal, such as the change we get when we keep an animal from sex activity, when we keep it from feeding, when we keep it from building a nest. By response we mean anything the animal does—such as turning toward or away from a light, jumping at a sound, and more highly organized activities such as building a skyscraper, drawing plans, having babies, writing books, and the like.

SOME SPECIFIC PROBLEMS OF THE BEHAVIORISTS

You will find, then, the behaviorist working like any other scientist. His sole object is to gather facts about behavior—verify his data—subject them both to logic and to mathematics (the tools of every scientist). He brings the new-born individual *into his experimental nursery* and begins to set problems: What is the baby doing now? What is the stimulus that makes him behave this way? He finds that the stimulus of tickling the cheek brings the response of turning the mouth to the side stimulated. The stimulus of the nipple brings out the sucking response. The stimulus of a rod placed on the palm of the hand brings closure of the hand and the suspension of the whole body by that hand and arm if the rod is raised. Stimulating the infant with a rapidly moving shadow across the eye will not produce blinking until the individual is sixty-five days of age. Stimulating the infant with an apple or stick of candy or any other object will not call out attempts at reaching until the baby is around 120 days of age. Stimulating a properly brought up infant at any age with snakes, fish, darkness, burning paper, birds, cats, dogs, monkeys, will not bring out that type of response which we call "fear" (which to be objective we might call reaction "X") which is a catching of the breath, a stiffening of the whole body, a turning away of the body from the source of stimulation, a running or crawling away from it.

On the other hand, there are just two things which will call out a fear response, namely, a loud sound, and loss of support.

Now the behaviorist finds from observing children brought up *outside of his nursery* that hundreds of these objects will call out fear responses. Consequently, the scientific question arises: If at birth only two stimuli will call out fear, how do all these other things ever finally come to call it out? Please note that the question is not a speculative one. It can be answered by experiments, and the experiments can be reproduced and the same findings can be had in every other laboratory if the original observation is sound. Convince yourself of this by making a simple test.

If you will take a snake, mouse or dog and show it to a baby who has never seen these objects or been frightened in other ways, he begins to manipulate it, poking at this, that or the other part. Do this for ten days until you are logically certain that the child will always go toward the dog and never run away from it (positive reaction) and that it does not call out a fear response at any time. In contrast to this, pick up a steel bar and strike upon it loudly behind the infant's head. Immediately the fear response is called forth. Now try this: At the instant you show him the animal and just as he begins to reach for it, strike the steel bar behind his head. Repeat the experiment three or four times. A new and important change is apparent. The animal now calls out the same response as the steel bar, namely a fear response. We call this, in behavioristic psychology, the *conditioned emotional response*—a form of *conditioned reflex*.

Our studies of conditioned reflexes make it easy for us to account for the child's fear of the dog on a thoroughly natural science basis without lugging in consciousness or any other so-called mental process. A dog comes toward the child rapidly, jumps upon him, pushes him down and at the same time barks loudly. Oftentimes one such combined stimulation is all that is necessary to make the baby run away from the dog the moment it comes within his range of vision.

There are many other types of conditioned emotional responses, such as those connected with *love*, where the mother by petting the child, rocking it, stimulating its sex organs in bathing, and the like, calls out the embrace, gurgling and crowing as an unlearned original response. Soon this response becomes conditioned. The mere sight of the mother calls out the same kind of response as actual bodily contacts. In *rage* we get a similar set of facts. The stimulus of holding the infant's moving members brings out the original unlearned response we call rage. Soon the mere sight of a nurse who handles a child badly throws the child into a fit. Thus we see how relatively simple our emotional responses are in the beginning and how terribly complicated home life soon makes them.

The behaviorist has his problems with the adult as well. What methods shall we use systematically to condition the adult? For example, to teach him business habits, scientific habits? Both manual habits (technique and skill) and laryngeal habits (habits of speech and thought) must be formed and tied together before the task of learning is complete. After these work habits are formed, what system of changing stimuli shall we surround him with in order to keep his level of efficiency high and constantly rising?

In addition to vocational habits, there comes the problem of his emotional life. How much of it is carried over from childhood? What part of it interferes with his present adjustment? How can we make him lose this part of it; that is, uncondition him where unconditioning is necessary, and condition him where conditioning is necessary? Indeed we know all too little about the amount and kind of emotional or, better, visceral habits (by this term we mean that our stomach, intestines, breathing, and circulation become conditioned—form habits) that should be formed. We do know that they are formed in large numbers and that they are important.

Probably more adults in this universe of ours suffer vicissitudes in family life and in business activities because of poor and insufficient visceral habits than through the lack of technique and skill in manual and verbal accomplishments. One of the large problems in big organizations today is that of personality adjustments. The young men and young women entering business organizations have plenty of skill to do their work but they fail because they do not know how to get along with other people.

NOTE

1In the last few decades there have been two other more or less prominent but temporary points of view—the so-called functional psychology of Dewey, Angell, and Judd, and the Gestalt Psychologie of Wertheimer, Koffka, and Köhler. In my opinion both of these points of view are, as it were, illegitimate children of introspective psychology. Functional psychology, which one rarely hears of now, owed its vogue to considerable patter about the physiologically adaptive functions of the mind. The mind with them is a kind of adjusting "guardian angel." The philosophy behind it smacks very much of the good old Christian philosophy of Berkeley (interaction or control of the body by the deity).

Gestalt psychology makes its patter about "configurational response (really inborn!)." As a psychological theory it cannot gain very much headway. It is as obscure as Kant's treatment of imagination, which it resembles quite a little. The kernel of truth behind it has been very much better and more clearly expressed by William James in his *Principles* in the chapters on Sensation and Perception. Those chapters could be read with profit by the sponsors of Gestalt. Gestalt is still a part of introspective psychology. Incidentally a bit of collateral reading for any student who works on Gestalt is Hobhouse's *Mind in Evolution*.

Clark L. Hull   (1884–1952)

Mind, Mechanism and Adaptive Behavior

Less hortatory than Watson but much more systematic and scholarly, Clark Hull transferred a youthful interest in engineering to the building of an intricate and ingenious "mathematico-deductive" structure of psychological theory. He resembled the engineer as well in his construction of what he called a "robot" model to test his firm belief that machines could be built which would duplicate the abilities of conscious human beings. Hull sought not only to rule out consciousness as a variable in the subject matter, but also to rule out empathy or identification with the subject (he called it "anthropomorphic subjectivism") on the part of the investigator. Human behavior was to be viewed as an automatic cyclical operation, each cycle commencing with the emergence of a "need" and ending with its abolition or reduction. The suggestion that there may be some aspects of human experience and conduct which could not be reduced to automatic mechanical processes was firmly dismissed by Hull as a "defeatist attitude" and a "doctrine of despair."*

The wide scope of Hull's influence is shown by his central role within the distinguished group of social and psychological scientists at the Yale Institute of Human Relations for a quarter of a century prior to his death. His greatest impact has been felt in the relatively new area

---

*Clark L. Hull, *Principles of Behavior: An Introduction to Behavior Theory* (New York: Appleton-Century, 1943), p. 26.

known as "learning theory"—of which the leading statement is to be found in a famous address delivered by Hull
as retiring president of the American Psychological Association in 1936, subsequently published as "Mind, Mechanism and Adaptive Behavior." The first part of that
essay is reproduced below.

SINCE THE TIME OF Charles Darwin it has become clear not
only that living organisms have gradually evolved through
immense periods of time, but that man is evolution's crown-
ing achievement. It is equally clear that man's pre-eminence
lies in his capacity for adaptive behavior. Because of the
seemingly unique and remarkable nature of adaptive behavior, it has long been customary to attribute it to the
action of a special agent or substance called "mind." Thus
"mind" as a hypothetical entity directing and controlling
adaptive behavior attains biological status possessing survival
value and, consequently, a "place in nature." But what is this
mysterious thing called mind? By what principle does it
operate? Are these principles many or are they few? Are they
those of the ordinary physical world or are they of the nature
of spiritual essences—of an entirely different order, the non-
physical?

It will, perhaps, be most economical to begin our examination of this important problem by passing briefly in review
some typical phenomena of adaptive behavior which have
led to the assumption of a special psychic entity. Among
these may be mentioned the following: When obstacles are
encountered, organisms often persist in making the same
incorrect attempt over and over again; they vary their reactions spontaneously; they display anticipatory reactions ante-
dating the biological emergencies to which the reactions
are adaptive; they present the phenomena of disappointment

and discouragement; they strive to attain states of affairs which are biologically advantageous; they transfer to new problem situations adaptive behavior acquired in situations which, objectively considered, are totally different. The behavior of organisms is purposive in that they strive for goals or values, and in so doing manifest intelligence or insight and a high degree of individual freedom from current coercion of the environment. Whatever may be the final conclusion as to the ultimate nature of these phenomena, their biological significance in terms of survival must be immense. The task of understanding and controlling them is surely worthy of the best cooperative efforts of the biological and social sciences.

THE CONTROVERSY REGARDING ADAPTIVE BEHAVIOR IS THEORETICAL, NOT FACTUAL

Historically, two main views have been held as to the ultimate nature of adaptive behavior. The most widely accepted of these, at the present time, is also the most ancient; its roots lie far back in primitive animism. According to this view, the principles governing adaptive behavor are essentially, non-physical, mental, or psychic. The second view, despite its austerity, has received a certain amount of favor among men of science. It assumes that adaptive behavior operates ultimately according to the principles of the physical world. In our consideration of these contrasting views, it will be convenient to begin with the latter.

The physical or mechanistic view of the nature of adaptive behavior can best be stated by quoting the beautiful presentation of the raindrop analogy written by the late Albert P. Weiss:

> We may best visualize the relationship between the responses that make up the so-called purposive behavior

category by the raindrop analogy. We may start with the
assumption that every drop of rain in some way or other
gets to the ocean. . . . Anthropomorphizing this condition
we may say that it is the *purpose* of every drop of rain to
get to the ocean. Of course, this only means that virtually
every drop *does* get there eventually. . . . Falling from the
cloud it may strike the leaf of a tree, and drop from one
leaf to another until it reaches the ground. From here it
may pass under or on the surface of the soil to a rill, then
to a brook, river, and finally to the sea. Each stage, each
fall from one leaf to the next, may be designated as a
means toward the final end, the sea, . . . Human behavior
is merely a complication of the same factors.[1]

The nub of Weiss's statement lies in his concluding remark that adaptive behavior is merely a "complication" of
the same factors as those which are involved in the behavior
of a drop of water finding its way from an inland cloud to
the sea. Obviously, Weiss did not mean to say that the several
forms of seeking and striving behavior characteristic of the
higher organisms are brought about by the various com-
poundings of such processes as evaporation, condensation,
splashing, and flowing. The context of the quotation shows
that he meant that ultimately the complex forms of purposive
behavior would be found to derive from the same *source*
as those from which the raindrop phenomena are derived;
i.e., from the basic entities of theoretical physics, such as
electrons and protons. He discusses these latter concepts
explicitly and at length.

Passing to the more orthodox view, that adaptive behavior
is essentially non-physical, or psychic, the words of A. S.
Eddington may be taken as a point of departure. In his book,
"The nature of the physical world,"[2] Eddington remarks:

Conceivably we might reach a human machine interacting
by reflexes with its environment; but we cannot reach
rational man morally responsible. . . . In a world of aether

and electrons we might perhaps encounter *nonsense*; we could not encounter *damned nonsense*.

The significance of Eddington's statement centers around the word *reach*. From the present point of view, he seems to be saying that we cannot reach the highest forms of adaptive behavior, such as complex problem solution (rational behavior) and certain complex forms of social behavior involving the implicit verbal coercion of the behavior of the individual (moral behavior) if we start out merely with aether and electrons; we must begin with something non-physical, or psychic—presumably consciousness.

Thus the issue is joined. We are presented with the paradox of Eddington, the physicist apparently insisting that the higher forms of behavior are at bottom non-physical, whereas Weiss, the psychologist, insists that they are fundamentally non-psychological!

But what, exactly, is the issue? Is it, for example, a difference as to an ordinary matter of observed fact? Do Eddington and those who share his view claim to have made certain observations which are in conflict with a corresponding set of observations supposed to have been made by Weiss and those with a mechanistic leaning? The dispute involves nothing of this nature. It is clear that the controversy is definitely a theoretical one. Eddington seems to be implying that we *can not* reach a sound theory of rational, purposive and moral behavior if we set out with nothing but aether and electrons. Weiss is saying, by implication, that a sound theory of such behavior *can* be reached by setting out with nothing but electrons and protons.

·　·　·

The essential characteristics of a sound scientific theoretical system, as contrasted with ordinary philosophical speculation, may be briefly summarized under three heads:

1. A satisfactory scientific theory should begin with a set of explicitly stated postulates accompanied by specific or "operational" definitions of the critical terms employed.

2. From these postulates there should be deduced by the most rigorous logic possible under the circumstances, a series of interlocking theorems covering the major concrete phenomena of the field in question.

3. The statements in the theorems should agree in detail with the observationally known facts of the discipline under consideration. If the theorems agree with the observed facts, the system is probably true; if they disagree, the system is false. If it is impossible to tell whether the theorems of a system agree with the facts or not, the system is neither true nor false; scientifically considered, it is meaningless.

NOTES

[1]Albert P. Weiss, *A Theoretical Basis of Human Behavior* (Columbus, Ohio: R. G. Adams and Company, 1925), pp. 346–347.

[2]New York: The Macmillan Company, 1929, p. 345.

B. F. Skinner   (1904–   )

The Problem of Control

Where Clark Hull sought to erect a predictive and "mathe-matico-deductive" science of behavior, B. F. Skinner has not hesitated to take the next step toward the anticipation of a science of human engineering and control. His scientific vision—at once psychological and cultural—has been spelled out systematically in a textbook, *Science and Human Behavior* (1953) and elaborated imaginatively in a novel, *Walden Two* (1948). More radical even than Watson and Pavlov in his objective behaviorism, Skinner has banished from his theoretical system concepts having to do with inner states or mental events. His experiments with both rats and pigeons, using his own invention, the "Skinner box," convinced him that the only differences between animals and men lie in the greater complexities of "verbal behavior." The result of this astringent appraisal of the human condition has been a forthright denial of the concept of freedom. "The hypothesis that man is not free," he has written, "is essential to the application of scientific method to the study of human behavior."* Elsewhere he has asserted as a "general principle that the issue of personal freedom must not be allowed to interfere with a scientific analysis of human behavior."† This combination

---

*B. F. Skinner, *Science and Human Behavior* (New York: Macmillan, 1953), p. 447.
†*Ibid.*, p. 315.

of disbelief in human liberty and devout faith in the power and glory of Science has led Skinner to assume the role of prophet (if not of propagandist) in the cause of the utopian community fictively portrayed in *Walden Two*. By 1967 there were at least two actual projects under way, in separate parts of the country, looking toward the establishment of such supposedly ideal communities. Something of the ethical frame of reference, as well as the scientific premises, of this design for group living may be gleaned from the following excerpt from *Science and Human Behavior*.

A POSSIBLE SAFEGUARD AGAINST DESPOTISM

THE ULTIMATE STRENGTH OF a controller depends upon the strength of those whom he controls. The wealth of a rich man depends upon the productivity of those whom he controls through wealth; slavery as a technique in the control of labor eventually proves nonproductive and too costly to survive. The strength of a government depends upon the inventiveness and productivity of its citizens; coercive controls which lead to inefficient or neurotic behavior defeat their own purpose. An agency which employs the stupefying practices of propaganda suffers from the ignorance and the restricted repertoires of those whom it controls. A culture which is content with the status quo—which claims to know what controlling practices are best and therefore does not experiment —may achieve a temporary stability but only at the price of eventual extinction.

By showing how governmental practices shape the behavior of those governed, science may lead us more rapidly to the design of a government, in the broadest possible sense, which will necessarily promote the well-being of those who are governed. The maximal strength of the manpower born to a group usually requires conditions which are described roughly with such terms as freedom, security, happiness, and knowledge. In the exceptional case in which it does not, the criterion of survival also works in the interests of the governed as well as those of the government. It may not be purely wishful thinking to predict that this kind of strength will eventually take first place in the considerations of those who engage in the design of culture. Such an achievement would simply represent a special case of self-control. . . . It is easy for a ruler, or the designer of a culture, to use any available power to achieve certain immediate effects. It is much more difficult to use power to achieve certain ultimate consequences. But every scientific advance which points up such consequences makes some measure of self-control in the design of culture more probable.

Government for the benefit of the governed is easily classified as an ethical or moral issue. This need not mean that governmental design is based upon any absolute principles of right and wrong but rather, as we have just seen, that it is under the control of long-term consequences. All the examples of self-control described [previously] could also be classified as ethical or moral problems. We deal with the ethics of governmental design and control as we deal with the ethics of any other sort of human behavior. For obvious reasons we call someone bad when he strikes us. Later, and for as obvious reasons, we call him bad when he strikes others. Eventually we object in more general terms to the use of physical force. Countermeasures become part of the ethical practices of our group, and religious agencies support these measures by branding the use of physical force immoral or sinful. All these measures which oppose the use of physical force are thus explained in terms of the immediate aversive consequences. In the design of government, we can, however, evaluate the use of physical force by considering the ultimate effect upon the group. Why should a particular government not slaughter the entire population of a captured city or country? It is part of our cultural heritage to call such behavior wrong and to react, perhaps in a violently emotional way, to the suggestion. The fact that the members of a group do react in this way could probably be shown to contribute ultimately to the strength of the group. But quite apart from such a reaction we may also condemn such a practice because it would eventually weaken the government. As we have seen, it would lead to much more violent resistance in other wars, to organized counterattack by countries afraid of meeting the same fate, and to very serious problems in the control of the government's own citizens. In the same way, although we may object to slavery because aversive control of one individual is also aversive to others, because it is "wrong," or because it is "incompatible with our conception of the dignity of man," an alternative consideration in the design of culture might be that slavery reduces the effectiveness of those who are enslaved and has serious effects upon other members of the group. Similarly, we defend a way of life which we believe to be superior to others by listing those characteristics which are immediately reinforcing to us and which we call ethically or morally good; but in evaluating a particular cultural experiment we may, instead, ask whether that way of life makes for the most effective development of those who follow it.

Ethical and moral principles have undoubtedly been valuable in the design of cultural practices. Presumably those principles which are with us today have been most valuable in this respect. However, the ultimate survival value of any given set is not thereby guaranteed. What science can tell us about the effect of a given practice upon behavior, and the effect of that behavior upon the survival of the group, may lead more directly to recognition of the ultimate strength of government in the broadest sense. Eventually the question must be asked with respect to mankind in general. Much has been written recently of the need to return to "moral law" in deliberations concerning human affairs. But the question, "Whose moral law?" frequently proves embarrassing. Faced with the problem of finding a moral law acceptable to all the peoples of the world, we become more acutely aware of the shortcomings of the principles proposed by any one group or agency. The possibility of promoting such principles, either through education or military conquest, is not promising. If a science of behavior can discover those conditions of life which make for the ultimate strength of men, it may provide a set of "moral values" which, because they are independent of the history and culture of any one group, may be generally accepted.

WHO WILL CONTROL?

Although science may provide the basis for a more effective cultural design, the question of who is to engage in such design remains unanswered. "Who *should* control?" is a spurious question—at least until we have specified the consequences with respect to which it may be answered. If we look to the long-term effect upon the group, the question becomes, "Who should control if the culture is to survive?" But this is equivalent to asking, "Who *will* control in the group which does survive?" The answer requires the kind of prediction which cannot be made with any certainty because of the extremely complex circumstances to be taken into account. In the long run, however, the most effective control from the point of view of survival will probably be based upon the most reliable estimates of the survival value of cultural practices. Since a science of behavior is concerned with demonstrating the consequences of cultural practices, we have some reason for believing that such a science will be an essential mark of the culture or cultures which survive. The current culture which, on this score alone, is most likely to survive is, therefore, that in which the methods of science are most effectively applied to the problems of human behavior.

This does not mean, however, that scientists are becoming self-appointed governors. It does not mean that anyone in possession of the methods and results of science can step outside the stream of history and take the evolution of government into his own hands. Science is not free, either. It cannot interfere with the course of events; it is simply part of that course. It would be quite inconsistent if we were to exempt the scientist from the account which science gives of human behavior in general. Science can, however, supply a description of the kind of process of which it itself is an example. A reasonable statement of our present position in the evolution of culture might take this form: We find ourselves members of a culture in which science has flourished and in which the methods of science have come to be applied to human behavior. If, as seems to be the case, the culture derives strength from this fact, it is a reasonable prediction that a science of behavior will continue to flourish and that our culture will make a substantial contribution to the social environment of the future.

THE FATE OF THE INDIVIDUAL

Western thought has emphasized the importance and dignity of the individual. Democratic philosophies of government, based upon the "rights of man," have asserted that all individuals are equal under the law, and that the welfare of the individual is the goal of government. In similar philosophies of religion, piety and salvation have been left to the individual himself rather than to a religious agency. Democratic literature and art have often been concerned with increasing man's knowledge and understanding of himself. Many schools of psychotherapy have accepted the philosophy that man is the master of his own fate. In education, social planning, and many other fields, the welfare and dignity of the individual have received first consideration.

The effectiveness of this point of view can scarcely be denied. The practices associated with it have strengthened the individual as an energetic and productive member of the group. The individual who "asserts himself" is one to whom the social environment is especially reinforcing. The environment which has characterized Western democratic thought has had this effect. The point of view is particularly important in opposition to despotic control and can, in fact, be countercontrol if a powerful agency is to strengthen the controllee. If the governing agency cannot be made to understand the value of the individual to the agency itself, the individual himself must be made to understand his own value. The effectiveness of the technique is evident in the fact that despotic governments have eventually been countercontrolled by individuals acting in concert to build a world which they find more reinforcing, and in the fact that governing agencies which recognize the importance of the individual have frequently become powerful.

The use of such concepts as individual freedom, initiative, and responsibility has, therefore, been well reinforced. When we turn to what science has to offer, however, we do not find very comforting support for the traditional Western point of view. The hypothesis that man is not free is essential to the application of scientific method to the study of human behavior. The free inner man who is held responsible for the behavior of the external biological organism is only a prescientific substitute for the kinds of causes which are discovered in the course of a scientific analysis. All these alternative causes lie *outside* the individual. The biological substratum itself is determined by prior events in a genetic process. Other important events are found in the nonsocial environment and in the culture of the individual in the broadest possible sense. These are the things which make the individual behave as he does. For them he is not responsible, and for them it is useless to praise or blame him. It does not matter that the individual may take it upon himself to control the variables of which his own behavior is a function or, in a broader sense, to engage in the design of his own culture. He does this only because he is the product of a culture which generates self-control or cultural design as a mode of behavior. The environment determines the individual even when he alters the environment.

This prior importance of the environment has slowly come to be recognized by those who are concerned with changing the lot of mankind. It is more effective to change the culture than the individual because any effect upon the individual as such will be lost at his death. Since cultures survive for much longer periods, any effect upon them is more reinforcing. There is a similar distinction between clinical medicine, which is concerned with the health of the individual, and the science of medicine, which is concerned with improving medical practices which will eventually affect the health of billions of individuals. Presumably, the emphasis on culture will grow as the relevance of the social environment to the behavior of the individual becomes clearer. We may therefore find it necessary to change from a philosophy which emphasizes the individual to one which emphasizes the culture or the group. But cultures also change and perish, and we must not forget that they are created by individual action and survive only through the behavior of individuals.

Science does not set the group or the state above the individual or vice versa. All such interpretations derive from an unfortunate figure of speech, borrowed from certain prominent instances of control. In analyzing the determination of human conduct we choose as a starting point a conspicuous link in a longer causal chain. When an individual conspicuously manipulates the variables of which the behavior of another individual is a function, we say that the first individual controls the second, but we do not ask who or what controls the first. When a government conspicuously controls its citizens, we consider this fact without identifying the events which control the government. When the individual is strengthened as a measure of countercontrol, we may, as in democratic philosophies, think of him as a starting point. Actually, however, we are not justified in assigning to anyone or anything the role of prime mover. Although it is necessary that science confine itself to selected segments in a continuous series of events, it is to the whole series that any interpretation must eventually apply.

Even so, the conception of the individual which emerges from a scientific analysis is distasteful to most of those who have been strongly affected by democratic philosophies. . . . It has always been the unfortunate task of science to dispossess cherished beliefs regarding the place of man in the universe. It is easy to understand why men so frequently flatter themselves—why they characterize the world in ways which reinforce them by providing escape from the consequences of criticism or other forms of punishment. But although flattery temporarily strengthens behavior, it is questionable whether it has any ultimate survival value. If science does not confirm the assumptions of freedom, initiative, and responsibility in the behavior of the individual, these assumptions will not ultimately be effective either as motivating devices or as goals in the design of culture. We may not give them up easily, and we may, in fact, find it difficult to control ourselves or others until alternative principles have been developed. But the change will probably be made. It does not follow that newer concepts will necessarily be less acceptable. We may console ourselves with the reflection that science is, after all, a cumulative progress in knowledge which is due to man alone, and that the highest human dignity may be to accept the facts of human behavior regardless of their momentary implications.

PART III

Person, Act, Existence:

Humanistic Psychology

.

William James (1842–1910)

The Stream of Consciousness

Still widely regarded half a century after his death as "America's foremost psychologist," William James stands out among his colleagues and successors both for his humanism and his humanness. He possessed an open-minded tolerance which welcomed intellectual movements as varied as physiological psychology and "psychic research." But it is well to remember that his youthful sympathy for such experimental pioneers as Helmholtz, Wundt, and Fechner had turned into exasperation by the time he published his classic work, *Principles of Psychology*, in 1890. As a sample of James's personality, as much as of his mature viewpoint, this account of what he termed the "microscopic psychology" of German experimentalism is worth recalling at some length:

This method taxes patience to the utmost, and hardly could have arisen in a country whose natives could be bored. Such Germans as Weber, Fechner, Vierordt and Wundt obviously cannot; and their success has brought into the field an array of younger experimental psychologists, bent on studying the elements of the mental life, dissecting them from the gross results in which they are embedded, and as far as possible reducing them to quantitative scales. The simple and open method of attack having done what it can, the method of patience, starving out, and harassing to death is tried; the Mind must submit to a regular siege, in which minute advantages gained night and day by the forces that hem her in must sum themselves up at last into her overthrow. There is little left of the grand style about

*these new prism, pendulum, and chronograph-philosophers. They
mean business, not chivalry. What generous divination, and that
superiority in virtue which was thought by Cicero to give a man
the best insight into nature, have failed to do, their spying and
scraping, their deadly tenacity and almost diabolic cunning, will
doubtless some day bring about.* *

One further quotation, this on Fechner and his psychophysics, is irresistible: "But it would be terrible if even
such a dear old man as this could saddle our Science forever with his patient whimsies, and, in a world so full of
more nutritious objects of attention, compel all future
students to plough through the difficulties, not only of his
own works, but of the still drier ones written in his refuta-
tion."† Both of these quotations as well as the main selection which follows are taken from James's *Principles,* a
monumental study some dozen years in the making, whose
enduring quality has been described by E. G. Boring: "In
the sixty years that have elapsed since its publication, its
vigor and freshness have remained undimmed, and its insight has refused to become anachronistic."‡ That insight
is well summed up in James's holistic treatment of the
"stream of thought" or consciousness, which illustrates his
repudiation of the elementistic reductionism of the Germans who dominated the field during the last quarter of
the century. In the first place, said James, consciousness
is an ongoing process, a "stream"; moreover, it is *personal,*
unique to a particular human being; and again it is a
continuously changing and developing affair. Perhaps most
important of all, he insisted that consciousness is an active
and *selective* process, involving the act of choice. "Action"
and "function" were the key terms in James's psychological
vocabulary, as indeed they came to be in the subsequent
development of his pragmatic philosophy.

---

*William James, *Principles of Psychology* (New York: Holt, 1890), vol. I,
pp. 192 f.

†*Ibid.,* vol. I, p. 549.

‡E. G. Boring, *A History of Experimental Psychology* (New York: Appleton-
Century-Crofts, Second Edition, 1950), p. 511.

In all of this, James, like John Dewey, is generally taken to be the very model of a modern Yankee scholar—practical, impatient of cant (or Kant), interested only in results: in a word, "American." But if that is true then most of academic psychology since James and Dewey has been un-American; for the prominent emphases of these functionalists upon the concept of the active self, upon the irreducible wholeness and configuration of the behavioral act and indeed of the person, and simply upon the responsibility and dignity of the human being, have found few echoes in the researches and writings of most American schools of thought in the intervening decades.

THE ORDER OF OUR study must be analytic. We are now prepared to begin the introspective study of the adult consciousness itself. Most books adopt the so-called synthetic method. Starting with "simple ideas of sensation," and regarding these as so many atoms, they proceed to build up the higher states of mind out of their "association," "integration," or "fusion," as houses are built by the agglutination of bricks. This has the didactic advantages which the synthetic method usually has. But it commits one beforehand to the very questionable theory that our higher states of consciousness are compounds of units; and instead of starting with what the reader directly knows, namely his total concrete states of mind, it starts with a set of supposed "simple ideas" with which he has no immediate acquaintance at all, and concerning whose alleged interactions he is much at the mercy of any plausible phrase. On every ground, then, the method of advancing from the simple to the compound exposes us to illusion. All pedants and abstractionists will naturally hate to abandon it. But a student who loves the fulness of human nature will prefer to follow the "analytic" method, and to begin with the most concrete facts, those with which he has a daily acquaintance in his own inner life. The analytic method will discover in due time the elementary parts, if such exist, without danger of precipitate assumption. The reader will bear in mind that our own chapters on sensation have dealt mainly with the physiological conditions thereof. They were put first as a mere matter of convenience, because incoming currents come first. *Psychologically* they might better have come last. Pure sensations were described as processes which in adult life are well-nigh unknown, and nothing was said which could for a moment lead the reader to suppose that they were the *elements of composition* of the higher states of mind.

THE FUNDAMENTAL FACT.—The first and foremost concrete fact which every one will affirm to belong to his inner experience is the fact that *consciousness of some sort goes on.* *"States of mind" succeed each other in him.* If we could say in English "it thinks," as we say "it rains" or "it blows," we should be stating the fact most simply and with the minimum of assumption. As we cannot, we must simply say that *thought goes on.*

FOUR CHARACTERS IN CONSCIOUSNESS.—How does it go on? We notice immediately four important characters in the process, of which it shall be the duty of the present chapter to treat in a general way:

(1) Every "state" tends to be part of a personal consciousness.

(2) Within each personal consciousness states are always changing.

(3) Each personal consciousness is sensibly continuous.

(4) It is interested in some parts of its objects to the exclusion of others, and welcomes or rejects—*chooses* from among them, in a word—all the while.

In considering these four points successively, we shall have to plunge *in medias res* as regards our nomenclature and use psychological terms which can only be adequately defined [later]. But every one knows what the terms mean in a rough way; and it is only in a rough way that we are now to take them. This chapter is like a painter's first charcoal sketch upon his canvas, in which no niceties appear.

When I say *every "state" or "thought" is part of a personal consciousness*, "personal consciousness" is one of the terms in question. Its meaning we know so long as no one asks us to define it, but to give an accurate account of it is the most difficult of philosophic tasks. . . .

In this room—this lecture-room, say—there are a multitude of thoughts, yours and mine, some of which cohere mutually, and some not. They are as little each-for-itself and reciprocally independent as they are all-belonging-together. They are neither: no one of them is separate, but each belongs with certain others and with none beside. My thought belongs with *my* other thoughts, and your thought with *your* other thoughts. Whether anywhere in the room there be a *mere* thought, which is nobody's thought, we have no means of ascertaining, for we have no experience of its like. The only states of consciousness that we naturally deal with are found in personal consciousnesses, minds, selves, concrete particular I's and you's.

Each of these minds keeps its own thoughts to itself. There is no giving or bartering between them. No thought even comes into direct *sight* of a thought in another personal consciousness than its own. Absolute insulation, irreducible pluralism, is the law. It seems as if the elementary psychic fact were not *thought* or *this thought* or *that thought*, but *my thought*, every thought being *owned*. Neither contemporaneity, nor proximity in space, nor similarity of quality and content are able to fuse thoughts together which are sundered by this barrier of belonging to different personal minds. The breaches between such thoughts are the most absolute breaches in nature. Every one will recognize this to be true, so long as the existence of *something* corresponding to the term "personal mind" is all that is insisted on, without any particular view of its nature being implied. On these terms the personal self rather than the thought might be treated as the immediate datum in psychology. The universal conscious fact is not "feelings and thoughts exist," but "I think" and "I feel." No psychology, at any rate, can question the *existence* of personal selves. Thoughts connected as we feel them to be connected are *what we mean* by personal selves. The worst a psychology can do is so to interpret the nature of these selves as to rob them of their *worth*.

CONSCIOUSNESS IS INCONSTANT CHANGE.—I do not mean by this to say that no one state of mind has any duration—even if true, that would be hard to establish. What I wish to lay stress on is this, that *no state once gone can recur and be identical with what it was before.* Now we are seeing, now hearing; now reasoning, now willing; now recollecting, now expecting; now loving, now hating; and in a hundred other ways we know our minds to be alternately engaged. But all these are complex states, it may be said, produced by combination of simpler ones;—do not the simpler ones follow a different law? Are not the *sensations* which we get from the same objects, for example, always the same? Does not the same piano-key, struck with the same force, make us hear in the same way? Does not the same grass give us the same feeling of green, the same sky the same feeling of blue, and do we not get the same olfactory sensation no matter how many times we put our nose to the same flask of cologne? It seems a piece of metaphysical sophistry to suggest that we do not;

and yet a close attention to the matter shows that *there is no proof that an incoming current ever gives us just the same bodily sensation twice.*

What is got twice is the same OBJECT. We hear the same *note* over and over again; we see the same *quality* of green, or smell the same objective perfume, or experience the same *species* of pain. The realities, concrete and abstract, physical and ideal, whose permanent existence we believe in, seem to be constantly coming up again before our thought, and lead us, in our carelessness, to suppose that our "ideas" of them are the same ideas. . . . How inveterate is our habit of simply using our sensible impressions as stepping-stones to pass over to the recognition of the realities whose presence they reveal. The grass out of the window now looks to me of the same green in the sun as in the shade, and yet a painter would have to paint one part of it dark brown, another part bright yellow, to give its real sensational effect. We take no heed, as a rule, of the different way in which the same things look and sound and smell at different distances and under different circumstances. The sameness of the *things* is what we are concerned to ascertain; and any sensations that assure us of that will probably be considered in a rough way to be the same with each other. This is what makes off-hand testimony about the subjective identity of different sensations well-nigh worthless as a proof of the fact. The entire history of what is called Sensation is a commentary on our inability to tell whether two sensible qualities received apart are exactly alike. What appeals to our attention far more than the absolute quality of an impression is its *ratio* to whatever other impressions we may have at the same time. When everything is dark a somewhat less dark sensation makes us see an object white. Helmholtz calculates that the white marble painted in a picture representing an architectural view by moonlight is, when seen by daylight, from ten to twenty thousand times brighter than the real moonlit marble would be.

Such a difference as this could never have been *sensibly* learned; it had to be inferred from a series of indirect considerations. These make us believe that our sensibility is altering all the time, so that the same object cannot easily give us the same sensation over again. We feel things differently accordingly as we are sleepy or awake, hungry or full, fresh or tired; differently at night and in the morning, differently in summer and in winter; and above all, differently in childhood, manhood, and old age. And yet we never doubt that our feelings reveal the same world, with the same sensible qualities and the same sensible things occupying it. The difference of the sensibility is shown best by the difference of our emotion about the things from one age to another, or when we are in different organic moods. What was bright and exciting becomes weary, flat, and unprofitable. The bird's song is tedious, the breeze is mournful, the sky is sad.

To these indirect presumptions that our sensations, following the mutations of our capacity for feeling, are always undergoing an essential change, must be added another presumption, based on what must happen in the grain. Every sensation corresponds to some cerebral action. For an identical sensation to recur it would have to occur the second time *in an unmodified brain*. But as this, strictly speaking, is a physiological impossibility, so is an unmodified feeling an impossibility; for to every brain-modification, however small, we suppose that there must correspond a change of equal amount in the consciousness which the brain subserves.

But if the assumption of "simple sensations" recurring in immutable shape is so easily shown to be baseless, how much more baseless is the assumption of immutability in the larger masses of our thought!

For there it is obvious and palpable that our state of mind is never precisely the same. Every thought we have of a given fact is, strictly speaking, unique, and only bears a resemblance of kind with our other thoughts of the same fact. When the identical fact recurs, we *must* think of it in a fresh manner, see it under a somewhat different angle, apprehend it in different relations from those in which it last appeared. And the thought by which we cognize it is the thought of it-in-those-relations, a thought suffused with the consciousness of all that dim context. Often we are ourselves struck at the strange differences in our successive views of the same thing. We wonder how we ever could have opined as we did last month about a certain matter. We have outgrown the possibility of that state of mind, we know not how. From one year to another we see things in new lights. What was unreal has grown real, and what was exciting is insipid. The friends we used to care the world for are shrunken to shadows; the women once so divine, the stars, the woods, and the waters, how now so dull and common!—the young girls that brought an aura of infinity, at present hardly distinguishable existences; the pictures so empty; and as for the books, what *was* there to find so mysteriously significant in Goethe, or in John Mill so full of weight? Instead of all this, more zestful than ever is the work, the work; and fuller and deeper the import of common duties and of common goods.

I am sure that this concrete and total manner of regarding the mind's changes is the only true manner, difficult as it may be to carry it out in detail. If anything seems obscure about it, it will grow clearer as we advance. Meanwhile, if it be true, it is certainly also true that no two "ideas" are ever exactly the same, which is the proposition we started to prove.

The proposition is more important theoretically than it at first sight seems. For it makes it already impossible for us to follow obediently in the footprints of either the Lockian or the Herbartian school, schools which have had almost unlimited influence in Germany and among ourselves. No doubt it is often *convenient* to formulate the mental facts in an atomistic sort of way, and to treat the higher states of consciousness as if they were all built out of unchanging simple ideas which "pass and turn again." It is convenient often to treat curves as if they were composed of small straight lines, and electricity and nerve-force as if they were fluids. But in the one case as in the other we must never forget that we are talking symbolically, and that there is nothing in nature to answer to our words. *A permanently existing "Idea" which makes its appearance before the footlights of consciousness at periodical intervals is as mythological an entity as the Jack of Spades.*

John Dewey (1859–1952)

The Reflex Arc Concept in Psychology

Like his senior and predecessor William James, John Dewey brilliantly combined the offices of psychologist and philosopher. Like James, also, he was a functionalist in the former role and a pragmatist in the latter. But these labels scarcely begin to touch the character and scope of Dewey's contributions to American thought and culture (and those of many other nations East and West) during an immensely productive lifetime which fell just seven years short of the century mark.

Born in the year in which *The Origin of Species* was published, Dewey became a "social Darwinist" of a kind very different from the Sumners and Spencers who exploited the theory of evolution to justify a jungle vision of competitive struggle and survival in the Gilded Age; for Dewey, evolution was a doctrine of progress and emergent intelligence, which preached not biological determinism and acquiescence but self-determination and active reform. Both in his psychology and his philosophy—which ranged across the board of speculation from ethics through politics to aesthetics—Dewey was primarily and persistently the spokesman for *change*. He was clearly the pre-eminent figure in that generation of intellectual and social reformers who, at the turn of the century, led a revolt against formalism and developed what has become known as the Progressive Scholarship—that "style of thinking," as Morton White has described it, "which dominated America for almost half a century—an intellectual pattern compounded of pragmatism, institutionalism, behaviorism, legal realism, economic determinism, the 'new history.' "* Among Dewey's peers in this progressive movement of thought were Justice Oliver Wendell Holmes and Roscoe Pound, Charles A. Beard and James Harvey Robinson, Thorstein Veblen and Lester Ward.

Something of the distinctive character of Dewey's approach to the field of psychology is suggested by the observation of Gordon W. Allport that Dewey, "more than any other scholar, past or present, has set forth as a psychological problem the common man's need to participate in his own destiny." To Dewey, life was not only action but interaction; the uses of mind were not only individual but social; the purpose of thought was not only the quest for certainty but the quest for community. His functionalism was a belief that intelligence was a human capacity to be used in the solution of human problems; himself a Middle Westerner, he embodied the practical frontier mentality which looked upon the world as a series of challenges to be sought out, coped with, and conquered. Mind in this view was no passive thing, helplessly twitching to the tune of every passing stimulus, but an active, organized, and creatively adaptive agent going out to meet the world and (in one way or another) to make it over. Thus in his epochal "position paper" of 1896, which defined the credo of the Chicago school of functionalism, Dewey attacked the prevailing "reflex arc concept in psychology"—with its reduction of human nature and conduct to the mechanical cycle of stimulus and response. The main point of Dewey's article was that the stimulus is not some simple prod or excitation but rather is the state of the total organism, the particular coordination of ongoing processes which constitutes a personal perspective. Behavior is therefore a selective, seriated, and organized action. "The stimulus,"

---

*Morton G. White, *Social Thought in America: The Revolt Against Formalism* (New York: Viking, 1949), p. 3.

as he later wrote, "is simply the earlier part of the total coordinated serial behavior and the response the latter part." This formulation conveys what Dewey termed the "correlativity of stimulus and response," in which attention or activity first determines the stimulus, and the stimulus in turn determines further activity—a notion which eventually led Dewey and his colleague George Herbert Mead to a theory of the mutual determination of form (organism) and environment.

LET US TAKE, FOR our example, the familiar child-candle instance. . . . The ordinary interpretation would say the sensation of light is a stimulus to the grasping as a response, the burn resulting is a stimulus to withdrawing the hand as response and so on. There is, of course, no doubt that is a rough practical way of representing the process. But when we ask for its psychological adequacy, the case is quite different. Upon analysis, we find that we begin not with a sensory stimulus, but with a sensori-motor coordination, the optical-ocular, and that in a certain sense it is the movement which is primary, and the sensation which is secondary, the movement of body, head and eye muscles determining the quality of what is experienced. In other words, the real beginning is with the act of seeing: it is looking, and not a sensation of light. The sensory quale gives the value of the act, just as the movement furnishes its mechanism and control, but both sensation and movement lie inside, not outside the act.

Now if this act, the seeing, stimulates another act, the reaching, it is because both of these acts fall within a larger coordination; because seeing and grasping have been so often bound together to reinforce each other, to help each other out, that each may be considered practically a subordinate member of a bigger coordination. More specifically, the ability of the hand to do its work will depend, either directly or indirectly, upon its control, as well as its stimulation, by the act of vision. If the sight did not inhibit as well as excite the reaching, the latter would be purely indeterminate, it would be for anything or nothing, not for the particular object seen. The reaching, in turn, must both stimulate and control the seeing. The eye must be kept upon the candle if the arm is to do its work; let it wander and the arm takes up another task. In other words, we now have an enlarged and transformed coordination; the act is seeing no less than before, but it is now seeing-for-reaching purposes. There is still a sensori-motor circuit, one with more content or value, not a substitution of a motor response for a sensory stimulus.

Now, take the affairs at its next stage, that in which the child gets burned. It is hardly necessary to point out again that this is also a sensori-motor coordination and not a mere sensation. It is worth while, however, to note especially the fact that it is simply the completion, or fulfillment, of the previous eye-arm-hand coordination and not an entirely new occurrence. Only because the heat-pain quale enters into the same circuit of experience with the optical-ocular and muscular quales, does the child learn from the experience and get the ability to avoid the experience in the future.

More technically stated, the so-called response is not merely *to* the stimulus; it is *into* it. The burn is the original seeing, the original optical-ocular experience enlarged and transformed in its value. It is no longer mere seeing; it is seeing-of-a-light-that-means-pain-when-contact-occurs. The ordinary reflex arc theory proceeds upon the more or less tacit assumption that the outcome of the response is a totally new experience; that it is, say, the substitution of a burn sensation for a light sensation through the intervention of motion. The fact is that the sole meaning of the intervening movement is to maintain, reinforce or transform (as the case may be) the original quale; that we do not have the replacing of one sort of experience by another, but the development . . . the mediation of an experience. The seeing, in a word, remains to control the reaching, and is, in turn, interpreted by the burning.

The discussion up to this point may be summarized by saying that the reflex arc idea, as commonly employed, is defective in that it assumes sensory stimulus and motor response as distinct psychical existences, while in reality they are always inside a coordination and have their significance purely from the part played in maintaining or reconstituting the coordination; and (secondly) in assuming that the quale of experience which precedes the "motor" phase and that which succeeds it are two different states, instead of the last being always the first reconstituted, the motor phase coming in only for the sake of such mediation. The result is that the reflex arc idea leaves us with a disjointed psychology, whether viewed from the standpoint of development in the individual or in the race, or from that of the analysis of the mature consciousness. As to the former, in its failure to see that the arc of which it talks is virtually a circuit, a continual reconstitution, it breaks continuity and leaves us nothing but a series of jerks, the origin of each jerk to be sought outside the process of experience itself, in either an external pressure of "environment," or else in an unaccountable spontaneous variation from within the "soul" or the "organism." As to the latter, failing to see the unity of activity, no matter how much it may prate of unity, it still leaves us with sensation or peripheral stimulus; idea, or central process (the equivalent of attention): and motor response, or act, as three disconnected existences, having to be somehow adjusted to each other, whether through the intervention of an extra-experimental soul, or by mechanical push and pull.

.   .   .

I hope it will not appear that I am introducing needless refinements and distinctions into what, it may be urged, is after all an undoubted fact, that movement as response follows sensation as stimulus. It is not a question of making the account of the process more complicated, though it is always wise to beware of that false simplicity which is reached by leaving out of account a large part of the problem. It is a question of finding out what stimulus or sensation, what movement and response mean; a question of seeing that they mean distinctions of flexible function only, not of fixed existence; that one and the same occurrence plays either or both parts, according to the shift of interest; and that because of this functional distinction and relationship, the supposed problem of the adjustment of one to the other, whether by superior force in the stimulus or an agency *ad hoc* in the center or the soul, is a purely self-created problem.

We may see the disjointed character of the present theory, by calling to mind that it is impossible to apply the phrase "sensori-motor" to the occurrence as a simple phrase of description; it has validity only as a term of interpretation, only, that is, as defining various functions exercised. In terms of description, the whole process may be sensory or it may be motor, but it cannot be sensori-motor. The "stimulus," the excitation of the nerve ending and of the sensory nerve, the central change, are just as much, or just as little, motion as the events taking place in the motor nerve and the muscles.

It is one uninterrupted, continuous redistribution of mass in motion. And there is nothing in the process, from the standpoint of description, which entitles us to call this reflex. It is redistribution pure and simple; as much so as the burning of a log, or the falling of a house or the movement of the wind. In the physical process, as physical, there is nothing which can be set off as stimulus, nothing which reacts, nothing which is response. There is just a change in the system of tensions.

The same sort of thing is true when we describe the process purely from the psychical side. It is now all sensation, all sensory quale; the motion, as psychically described, is just as much sensation as is sound or light or burn. Take the withdrawing of the hand from the candle flame as example. What we have is a certain visual-heat-pain-muscular-quale, transformed into another visual-touch-muscular-quale —the flame now being visible only at a distance, or not at all, the touch sensation being altered, etc. . . . The motion is not a certain kind of existence; it is a sort of sensory experience interpreted, just as is candle flame, or burn from candle flame. All are on a par.

But, in spite of all this, it will be urged, there is a distinction between stimulus and response, between sensation and motion. Precisely; but we ought now to be in a condition to ask of what nature is the distinction, instead of taking it for granted as a distinction somehow lying in the existence of the facts themselves. We ought to be able to see that the ordinary conception of the reflex arc theory, instead of being a case of plain science, is a survival of the metaphysical dualism, first formulated by Plato, according to which the sensation is an ambiguous dweller on the border land of soul and body, the idea (or central process) is purely psychical, and the act (or movement) purely physical. Thus the reflex arc formulation is neither physical (or physiological) nor psychological; it is a mixed materialistic-spiritualistic assumption.

If the previous descriptive analysis has made obvious the need of a reconsideration of the reflex arc idea, of the nest of difficulties and assumptions in the apparently simple statement, it is now time to undertake an explanatory analysis. The fact is that stimulus and response are not distinctions of existence, but teleological distinctions, that is, distinctions of function, or part played, with reference to reaching or maintaining an end. With respect to this teleological process, two stages should be discriminated, as their confusion is one cause of the confusion attending the whole matter. In one case, the relation represents an organization of means with reference to a comprehensive end. It represents an accomplished adaptation. Such is the case in all well developed instincts, as when we say that the contact of eggs is a stimulus to the hen to set; or the sight of corn a stimulus to pick; such also is the case with all thoroughly formed habits, as when the contact with the floor stimulates walking. In these instances there is no question of consciousness of stimulus *as* stimulus, of response *as* response. There is simply a continuously ordered sequence of acts, all adapted in themselves and in the order of their sequence, to reach a certain objective end, the reproduction of the species, the preservation of life, locomotion to a certain place. The end has got thoroughly organized into the means. In calling one stimulus, another response we mean nothing more than that such an orderly sequence of acts is taking place. The same sort of statement might be made equally well with reference to the succession of changes in a plant, so far as these are considered with reference to their adaptation to, say, producing seed. It is equally applicable to the series of events in the circulation of the blood, or the squence of acts occurring in a self-binding reaper.

William Stern (1871–1938)

Psychology from the Personalistic Standpoint

William Stern, who received his Ph.D. at the University of Berlin in 1892 and had been teaching before the turn of the century, was reportedly presiding at a meeting of the German Psychological Society in the early 1930's when a Hitler functionary arrived and ordered him to vacate the chair. Subsequently, as a member of that extraordinary generation of German scholars and intellectuals in exile, Stern joined the faculty of Duke University at the behest of a fellow humanist in psychology, William McDougall. Ironically, both Stern and McDougall died within months of each other, at the same age, in 1938.

Stern possessed more than a single claim to enduring recognition. In 1911 he introduced the Intelligence Quotient (I.Q.) as a device for the quantitative assessment of intelligence; and his early work in educational and developmental psychology influenced such pioneer child psychologists as Piaget. But his greatest achievement was his establishment of the personalistic approach to the study of man —which on its philosophical side he called "personalism" and on its psychological side "personalistics." Like Fechner, Wundt, Jaspers, and others who were products of the rounded humanistic education available at the great European universities of that period, Stern was as much at home in philosophy as in psychology; among his works is a three-volume philosophical study, *Person und Sache* (*Person and Thing*).

His personalistic psychology first became generally known to Americans through a 1937 article by Gordon W. Allport, "The Personalistic Psychology of William Stern," followed the next year by the English translation of his major work, *General Psychology from the Personalistic Standpoint.* His viewpoint was summed up in the statement that "the person is a living whole, individual, unique, striving toward goals, self-contained and yet open to the world around him; he is capable of having experience." In the emphasis on goal-directed striving, Stern was allied with his colleague McDougall; in the emphasis upon the human person as a whole and unique being, he was the forerunner of such theorists as Maslow, Rogers, Allport, Murray, Angyal, Murphy, and others of the contemporary "Third Force" movement. And in his stress upon holism and openness to the world, Stern anticipated both the Gestaltists and the neo-Freudians. (It was Stern, however, who admonished the former group that "there can be no Gestalt without a Gestalter!")

THE SUBSTRATUM OF MIND

In the opening pages of this book the subject-matter of *all* psychology was designated in a twofold way as embracing the essential nature and activity of mind. Or in more general terms, the *substratum* and the *empirical facts* of mind. It was also stated . . . that these two aspects cannot be studied independently of each other; they are mutually conditioned. The manner of conceiving the substratum of mind necessarily gives direction to the psychological study of mental data and makes possible explanation and interpretation of the empirical phenomena.

1. Introductory Questions

Do mental data have any "substratum"? Is there an entity *by which* they are substantiated and *from which* they issue?

The question must be answered in the affirmative. In itself mentality is only a state of being or attribute, and not an entity. (That is why we purposely prefer the *adjectival* terms "psychical" and "mental" in order to express this contingent, "inherent" character.)

The attempt has often been made to deny a substratum to mind or at least to exclude it from all scientific investigation. In consequence the contents of mind as such were substantialized; ideas, conations, character traits, instincts, etc. were treated as entities that somewhere and somehow had existence, and supposedly dangled in space. This view disregarded the fact that within psychological experience itself —quite independently, thus far, of philosophical hypotheses —mental phenomena, processes, and states are simply *properties* of the concomitant individual self that "has" them. Not the existence of a substratum but only its *nature* is open to question.

Is the substratum to be thought of as an independent "soul"? This second question signifies: Does the substratum itself belong to the mental category? Does its sole essence consist in generating, in owning, in governing the mental realm? And is the substratum accordingly to be contrasted with the individual's non-mental being, with his body, as with something different and alien? This question is answered in the negative.

The assumption of a substantial mind would require (*a*) that the *mentality* of the individual, as the product of his mind, comprise a closed system of interrelations, (*b*) that the *individual* represent a substantial duality of mind and body, (*c*) that the relationships *between* mind and body be secondary as compared with the primary relationships that hold *within* each category, (*d*) that everything subsisting and taking place in the individual come *wholly* under the heading of mind on the one hand or of body on the other.

. . . As one existing counter-proposal we find the extreme view of materialism, which holds that material substance is the only reality; the substratum of what is called mind is simply the body; mind is constituted by physiological, bodily processes. It is not necessary to restate here the frequently reiterated philosophical arguments against materialism. *Psychology* disposes of it with indirect but telling contrary evidence: its own existence. There *is* a science of mind, and this science deals with something quite different from physiological processes that have been, as it were, merely translated into other terms; it deals with internal experience and events and the ability to have experience; and these categories are different from those of the purely physical world.

There remains but one possibility: The substratum of mind must be something *that has existence going beyond or prior to the differentiation into the mental and the physical*, thereby certifying the original unity of the individual. This formula sounds "monistic," for all monism attacks the substantial duality of *physics* and *psyche*, viewing both simply as characteristics of a single substrate (thus Spinoza: "Thought and extension are attributes of the sole substance."). But current monism neglects the question as to the *nature* of the substratum, for this is defined merely as being "at once physical and psychical"; other specifications are not admitted or pass for unknowable. Consequently monism remains on the same plane that was supposedly transcended by its denial of the duality, and it must rest content with affirming the persisting coexistence of the two disparate attributes ("parallelism") without being able to grasp the *meaning* of this correlation.

There remains the crucial question as to whether the substratum may be defined by *positive* criteria that in themselves belong neither to the purely psychical nor to the purely physical sphere; in other words, whether the categories "physical" and "psychical" can themselves be subordinated as secondary to another category that appropriately defines its essential nature. The affirmation of this view is the fundamental task of the personalistic theory. Not only from the philosophical point of view is the person a "psychophysically neutral" being, but he may also be characterized and *empirically* apprehended through qualities that exist apart from the differentiation into body and mind.

2. *Definitions*

We define the person as follows:

The "person" is a living whole, individual, unique, striving toward goals, self-contained and yet open to the world around him; he is capable of having experience.

Except for the criterion of "experiencing," which was purposely placed at the end, the specifications throughout are *psychophysically neutral.* Into the totality of the person are interwoven both his physical and psychical aspects. Goal-directed activity is manifested in breathing and limb movements as well as in thinking and striving. Independence of and exposure to the environment apply both to bodily functions and to conscious phenomena.

The attribute "capable of having experience" is distinct from all the others in that it is *non-compulsory.* Every person *must* be at all times and in all respects a totality possessing life, individual uniqueness, goal-directed activity, independence of and openness to the world, *but not always consciousness.* Even at times when nothing is being "experienced" the person exists, while the loss of any one of the other attributes would suspend existence.

There is a *science* of the human "person," that studies

him in his totality and psychophysical neutrality; it is *personalistics*. It furnishes common hypotheses for all specialized scientific studies of the person: for the biology, the physiology, the pathology, the psychology, of the person. *Psychology is the science of the person as having experience or as capable of having experience.* It studies this personal attribute, experience, in regard to the conditions of its appearance, its nature, mode of functioning and regularity, and its significance for personal existence and life considered as a whole.

Kurt Koffka (1886–1941)

Perception and Gestalt Psychology

The twentieth-century movement which has come to be known as Gestalt (earlier called in English "configurationism") was a systematic protest against the German tradition of experimental psychology with its reduction of behavior and experience into atomistic elements and their associations. The first premonitory signal of the movement to come was sounded earlier by C. von Ehrenfels, who had noted that when two series of notes were played in two sets of keys, they produced the same melody—not, as elemantarism would require, two different melodies. Evidently, as William James pointed out, the pattern or whole of the song was more than the additive sum of the parts. These rebellious considerations were reinforced in 1912 when Wertheimer's investigations into the perception of apparent movement of lines gave rise to the concept of the phiphenomenon—a visual impression of movement which cannot be traced to the objective stimulus or further reduced into constituent elements or sensations. What Wertheimer was verifying was the capacity of the mind to make visual wholes out of actual parts, to order and arrange the perceived world in patterned terms.

On the basis of these researches, a singular trio of German psychologists set out, as J. C. Flügel has put it, "to wage war on the elementarist-associationist psychology." Wertheimer's colleagues at the University of Berlin included Kurt Koffka and Wolfgang Köhler, each of whom went on in a particular direction to construct the school of Gestalt

149

psychology. It was Köhler whose famous experiments with
the learning ability of apes, demonstrating the presence of
"insight" into a "whole" situation, had a profound impact
upon the course of educational and developmental psychology—reversing the old fashion of beginning all lessons
with elementary units and combining them gradually into
wholes. Koffka took the lead in challenging the entire tradition of trial-and-error learning; and indeed, as Roback
has noted, "Gestaltism opposed itself mainly to every form
of behaviorism" at the very time when the latter school of
thought was at the height of fashion. The Gestaltists
brought to the intellectual contest a sense of the organic as
against the mechanical, an appreciation of the whole as
distinct from and superior to its parts, an awareness of
synthesis as well as of analysis, and an insistence upon the
role of *value* in human experience and conduct.

To be sure, the "Gestalt revolution" was not revolutionary enough to admit the perceiver into perceptual theory
or the person into behavior theory. The Gestaltists did
add to the stimulus-object of S-R psychology another set
of forces of a neural and physiological character within
the responding subject (specifically within the brain); and
perceptual behavior became the product of their interaction. Hence in effect (if unintentionally) the conscious
person as an active agent in his own conduct was not much
less ignored by the Gestaltists than by their antagonists of
the mechanistic persuasion. But if the configurational psychologists were scarcely personalists in their theory, they
were surely humanists in their resistance to the prevailing
experimentalist fragmentation of the perceiving and behaving subject of psychology.

The selection which follows is taken from Koffka's "Perception: An Introduction to the *Gestalt-Theorie*."

W~HEN IT WAS SUGGESTED~ to me that I should write a general
critical review of the work recently carried on in the field
of perception, I saw an opportunity of introducing to Ameri-

can readers a movement in psychological thought which has developed in Germany during the last ten years. In 1912 Wertheimer stated for the first time the principles of a *Gestalt-Theorie* which has served as the starting point of a small number of German psychologists. Wherever this new method of thinking and working has come in touch with concrete problems, it has not only showed its efficiency, but has also brought to light startling and important facts, which, without the guidance of this theory, could not so easily have been discovered.

The *Gestalt-Theorie* is more than a theory of perception: it is even more than a mere psychological theory. Yet it originated in a study of perception, and the investigation of this topic has furnished the better part of the experimental work which has been done. Consequently, an introduction to this new theory can best be gained, perhaps, by a consideration of the facts of perception.

Since the new point of view has not yet won its way in Germany, it is but fair to state at the outset that the majority of German psychologists still stands aloof. However, much of the work done by other investigators contains results that find a place within the scope of our theory. Accordingly I shall refer to these results as well as to those secured by the *Gestalt*-psychologists proper; for I wish to demonstrate the comprehensiveness of our theory by showing how readily it embraces a number of facts hitherto but imperfectly explained. For the same reason I shall occasionally go farther back and refer to older investigations. On the other hand, I cannot hope to give a complete survey of the work on perception, and I shall therefore select my facts with reference to my primary purpose.

Since my chief aim is to invite a consideration of the new theory, I shall try first of all to make my American readers understand what the theory purports to be. So far there exists no general presentation of the theory which marshals all the facts upon which it rests; indeed, the general field of psychology has not, as yet, been treated from this point of view. For this reason the understanding of the theory has met with serious difficulties, and numerous misunderstandings have occasioned a great deal of the disapprobation which the theory has met. And yet, a theory which has admittedly inspired so many successful investigations may surely claim the right to be at least correctly understood.

My plan in detail is the following: After giving a short sketch of the chief concepts of current psychology as they present themselves to the mind of a *Gestalt*-psychologist, I shall introduce the newer concepts by demonstrating how appropriate they are in the solution of a very old psychological problem. I shall then proceed by developing a fundamental distinction made by the new theory which is quite contrary to the traditional view, and I shall also show the wide application of this distinction. . . .

When I speak of perception in the following essay, I do not mean a specific psychical function; all I wish to denote by this term is the realm of experiences which are not merely "imagined," "represented," or "thought of." Thus, I would call the desk at which I am now writing a perception, likewise the flavor of the tobacco I am now inhaling from my pipe, or the noise of the traffic in the street below my window. That is to say, I wish to use the term perception in a way that will exclude all theoretical prejudice; for it is my aim to propose a theory of these everyday perceptions which has been developed in Germany during the last ten years, and to contrast this theory with the traditional views of psychology. With this purpose in mind, I need a term that is quite neutral. In the current textbooks of psychology the term perception is used in a more specific sense, being opposed to sensation, as a more complex process. Here, in-deed, is the clue to all the existing theories of perception which I shall consider in this introductory section, together with a glance at the fundamental principles of traditional psychology. Thus I find three concepts, involving three principles of psychological theory, in every current psycho-logical system. In some systems these are the only fundamental concepts, while in others they are supplemented by addition-al conceptions; but for a long time the adequacy of these three has been beyond dispute. The three concepts to which I refer are those of *sensation, association,* and *attention.* I shall formulate the theoretical principles based upon these concepts and indicate their import in a radical manner so as to lay bare the methods of thinking which have been employed in their use. I am fully aware, of course, that most, if not all, the writers on this subject have tried to modify the assertions which I am about to make; but I maintain, nevertheless, that in working out concrete problems these principles have been employed in the manner in which I shall state them.

1. Sensation: All present or existential consciousness con-sists of a finite number of real, separable (though not neces-sarily separate) elements, each element corresponding to a definite stimulus or to a special memory-residuum (see below). Since a conscious unit is thus taken to be a bundle of such elements, Wertheimer, in a recent paper on the founda-tions of our new theory, has introduced the name "bundle-hypothesis" for this conception. These elements, or rather, some of them, are the sensations, and it is the first task of psychology to find out their number and their properties.

The elements, once aroused in the form of sensations, may also be experienced in the form of images. The images are also accepted as elements or atoms of psychological textures

and are distinguishable from sensations by certain characteristic properties. They are, however, very largely a dependent class, since every image presupposes a corresponding
sensation. Thus the concept of image, though not identical
with that of sensation, rests upon the same principle, namely,
the bundle-hypothesis.

In accordance with the method by which sensations have
been investigated, it has been necessary to refer to the
stimulus-side in defining the principle which underlies this
concept. More explicitly, this relation of the sensation to its
stimulus is expressed by a generally accepted rule, termed by
Köhler the "constancy-hypothesis"; that the sensation is a
direct and definite function of the stimulus. Given a certain
stimulus and a normal sense-organ, we know what sensation
the subject must have, or rather, we know its intensity and
quality, while its "clearness" or its "degree of consciousness"
is dependent upon still another factor, namely, *attention*.

What the stimulus is to the sensation, the residuum is to
the image. Since each separate sensation-element leaves behind it a separate residuum, we have a vast number of these
residua in our memory, each of which may be separately
aroused, thus providing a certain independence of the original arrangement in which the sensations were experienced.
This leads to the theory of the "association mixtures" (*associative Mischwirkungen*) propounded by G. E. Müller
and carried to the extreme in a paper by Henning.

2. Association: Even under our first heading we have met
with the concept of memory. According to current teaching,
the chief working principle of memory is association, although the purest of associationists recognize that it is not
the only principle. It may suffice to point out in this connection that Rosa Heine concludes from experiments performed in G. E. Müller's laboratory, that recognition is not

based upon association; for she failed to detect in recognition any trace of that retroactive inhibition which is so powerful a factor in all associative learning. Likewise, Müller himself, relying upon experiments by L. Schluter, as acknowledges the possibility of reproduction by similarity. Yet, despite all this, association holds its position as the primary factor governing the coming and the going of our ideas, and the law of association is based upon the sensation-image concept. Our train of thought having been broken up into separate elements, the question is asked by what law does one element cause the appearance of another, and the answer is, association, the tie that forms between each element and all those other elements with which it has ever been in contiguity. As Wertheimer again has pointed out, the core of this theory is this, that the necessary and sufficient cause for the formation and operation of an association is an original existential connection—the mere coexistence of *a* and *b* gives to each a tendency to reproduce the other. Meaning, far from being regarded as one of the conditions of association, is explained by the working of associations, which in themselves are meaningless.

Another feature of this theory is its statistical nature. At every moment, endless associations are working, reinforcing and inhibiting each other. Since we can never have a complete survey of all the effective forces, it is impossible in any single case to make accurate prediction. As the special laws of association can be discovered by statistical methods only, so our predictions can be only statistical.

3. Attention: It is a recognized fact, that, clear and simple as association and sensation appear to be, there is a good deal of obscurity about the concept of attention. And yet, wherever there is an effect that cannot be explained by sensation or association, there attention appears upon the stage. In more complex systems attention is the makeshift, or the

scapegoat, if you will, which always interferes with the working out of these other principles. If the expected is applied, attention to other contents must have caused it to pass unnoticed, or if a sensation does not properly correspond to the stimulus applied, the attention must have been inadequate, thus leading us to make a false judgment. We meet with like instances over and over again which justify the following general statement, that attention must be added as a separate factor which not only influences the texture and the course of our conscious processes, but is also likely to be influenced by them.

Modern psychology has endeavored to give a physiological foundation to its psychological conceptions. Let us therefore glance at the physiological side of these three principles. The substratum of sensation (and image) is supposed to be the arousal of a separate and circumscribed area of the cortex, while the substratum for association is the neural connection established between such areas. Again attention holds an ambiguous position, for some see its essence as a facilitation and some as an inhibition of the nervous processes. Without going more into detail, let us examine the nature of this psychophysical correspondence. Methodologically the physiological and the psychological aspects of these three principles are in perfect harmony; the cortex has been divided into areas, the immediate experience has been analyzed into elements, and connections are assumed to exist between brain areas as between the elements of consciousness. Furthermore, the nervous processes may be altered functionally and their corresponding psychological elements are subject to the functional factor of attention. Evidently the psychological and the physiological are interdependent, and are not sensation, association, and attention, factual? Do not cortical areas exist, and likewise nervous tracts, and the facilitation and inhibition of excitations? Certainly facts exist which have been interpreted in these ways, but we believe it can be proved that this interpretation is insufficient in the face of other and more comprehensive facts. Furthermore, we maintain that the insufficiency of the older theory cannot be remedied by supplementing the three principles, but that these must be sacrificed and replaced by other principles. It is not a discovery of the *Gestalt-psychologie* that these three concepts are inadequate to cover the abundance of mental phenomena, for many others have held the same opinion, and some have even begun experimental work with this in mind. I need but mention v. Ehrenfels and the Meinong school as one instance, Kulpe and the Wurzburg school as another. But they all left the traditional concepts intact, and while trying to overcome the difficulties by the expedient of adding new concepts, they could not check the tendency involved in these new concepts to modify the old ones. I must, however, warn the reader not to confound the old term of *Gestalt-Qualitat* with the term *Gestalt* as it is employed in the new theory. It was to avoid this very confusion that Wertheimer in his first paper avoided the term and introduced a totally neutral expression for the perception of movement—the *phi-phenomenon.*

Gordon W. Allport (1897–   )

Becoming: The Dilemma of Uniqueness

Something of the stature of the American personality psychologist Gordon W. Allport is indicated by the fact that, in a poll of practicing clinical psychologists by the American Psychological Association, only the name of Freud appeared before that of Allport in terms of degree of influence upon their day-to-day clinical work. This finding is the more significant when it is recognized that Allport, unlike Freud, is not a builder of monumental systems of theory and therapy; nor is he, unlike such other influential Americans as Hull and Skinner, a rigorous experimentalist or technician with a passion for logical perfection or empirical exactitude. His published work— ranging over forty years in time and almost as many fields in scope—demonstrates a consistent commitment to the affirmative conception of the human person as a unique whole, to be understood in idiographic (personal-history) terms rather than in those of nomothetic generalization and classification. Moreover, for Allport, each personality is an *open* rather than a *closed* system of dynamic organization—open to the world and to social encounter, free to act upon that world through the execution of purposes and choices, not merely to be pushed about by its fates and forces. Like James and Dewey before him, Allport projects an essentially optimistic psychology of normality; in his view men for the most part are not crippled by the biological legacy of appetites nor overborne

159

by the acquired incubus of superego inhibitions. Men at some time are masters of their fates; and when they are not, the fault is not in their stars but in themselves, and therefore correctible. This broadly affirmative and constructive quality of Allport's psychology has been given explicit expression in the epilogue to his classic essay, *Becoming: Basic Considerations for a Psychology of Personality*, which was based upon the Terry Lectures delivered at Yale in 1954 and from which our main selection as well is taken:

> *I have written this essay because I feel that modern psychology is in a dilemma. Broadly speaking, it has trimmed down the image of man that gave birth to the democratic dream. . . .*
>
> *Up to now the "behavioral sciences," including psychology, have not provided us with a picture of man capable of creating or living in a democracy. . . . They have delivered into our hands a psychology of an "empty organism," pushed by drives and molded by environmental circumstance. . . . But the theory of democracy requires also that man possess a measure of rationality, a portion of freedom, a generic conscience, propriate ideals, and unique value. We cannot defend the ballot box or liberal education, nor advocate free discussion and democratic institutions, unless man has the potential capacity to profit therefrom.* *

PERSONALITY IS LESS A finished product than a transitive process. While it has some stable features, it is at the same time continually undergoing change. It is this course of change, of becoming, of individuation that is now our special concern.

The first fact that strikes us is the uniqueness of both the process and the product. Each person is an idiom unto himself, an apparent violation of the syntax of the species. An idiom develops in its own peculiar context, and this context must be understood in order to comprehend the idiom. Yet

---

*Gordon W. Allport, *Becoming: Basic Considerations for a Psychology of Personality* (New Haven: Yale, 1955), pp. 99–100.

at the same time, idioms are not entirely lawless and arbitrary; indeed they can be known for what they are only by comparing them with the syntax of the species.

Now the scientific training of the psychologist leads him to look for universal processes common to the species, and to neglect the idiomatic pattern of becoming. While he may *say* that his subject matter is human personality, his habits lead him to study mind-in-general rather than mind-in-particular.

It is not that the psychologist is uninterested in John, the person. It is merely that his habits of thought lead him to ablate from John's nature some single segment for study. The surgery is accomplished by impressing upon John certain universal cutting instruments. One incision has to do, shall we say, with the "need for achievement," another with the "intelligence quotient." These incisions are not viewed as intersecting one another in John but rather as intersecting corresponding properties in other persons. The result is that we usually view John's personality as a diagram in a set of external co-ordinates, having no interrelations, no duration in time, no motion, no life, no variability, no uniqueness. What is peculiarly Johnian our methods of analysis do not tell.

It is true that the branch of psychology called "clinical" hopes somehow to bring about a coincidence of John with the properties abstracted from him. It endeavors to reclaim him from the sea of statistical averages. But for two reasons it runs into trouble. In the first place, as we have said, the universal dimensions employed in diagnosing John may be irrelevant to his personality. Perhaps he has no "need for achievement" but only a peculiar and unique need for exhibitionistic domination. The dimension employed seriously misses the precise coloring of his motivation. In the second place, we have few tools as yet to determine the mutual interrelations of dimensions. Thus we discover only that John stands at the tenth percentile on "need achievement," at the fiftieth in ability at "spatial manipulation," at the eighty-first percentile on "common responses" to the Rorschach test. Such bits of information comprise most clinical reports. Seldom do these bits of information intersect one another. We are still in the dark concerning the nexus of John's life. A large share of our trouble lies in the fact that the elements we employ in our analyses are not true parts of the original whole.

It is not helpful, I think, to reply that science, by its very nature, is impotent in the face of the idiomatic process of becoming. If there is to be a science of personality at all it should do better than it has in the past with the feature of personality that is most outstanding—its manifest uniqueness of organization.

Nor is it helpful to take refuge in the example of other sciences. We are told that every stone in the field is unique, every old shoe in the closet, every bar of iron, but that this ubiquitous individuality does not affect the operations or the progress of science. The geologist, the physicist, the cobbler proceed to apply universal laws, and find the accident of uniqueness irrelevant to their work. The analogy is unconvincing. Stones, old shoes, bars of iron are purely reactive; they will not move unless they are manipulated. They are incapable of becoming. How is it then with uniqueness in the realm of biology where in addition to reactivity each plant manifests the capacities for self-repair, self-regulation, adaptation? One leaf on the tree is large, another small, one deformed, another healthy. Yet all obey the sure laws of metabolism and cell structure. It is only in our aesthetic moments that we are interested in the precise shape, size, form, or individuality of a given leaf, plant, or animal.

But here too the analogy is weak. Unlike plants and lower animals, man is not merely a creature of cell structure, tropism, and instinct; he does not live his life by repeating, with trivial variation, the pattern of his species. Nature's heavy investment in individuality stands forth chiefly in *homo sapiens*. While we may recognize individual differences among dogs or varying strains of temperament among rats, still their lives in all essential particulars are regulated by their membership in a species. Man alone has the capacity to vary his biological needs extensively and to add to them countless psychogenic needs reflecting in part his culture (no other creature has a culture), and in part his own style of life (no other creature worries about his life-style).

Hence the individuality of man extends infinitely beyond the puny individuality of plants and animals, who are primarily or exclusively creatures of tropism or instinct. Immense horizons for individuality open when billions of cortical cells are added to the meager neural equipment of lower species. Man talks, laughs, feels bored, develops a culture, prays, has a foreknowledge of death, studies theology, and strives for the improvement of his own personality. The infinitude of resulting patterns is plainly not found in creatures of instinct. For this reason we should exercise great caution when we extrapolate the assumptions, methods, and concepts of natural and biological science to our subject matter. In particular we should refuse to carry over the indifference of other sciences to the problem of individuality.

Emulation of an older science never creates a newer science. It is only unquenchable curiosity about some persistent phenomenon of nature that does so. Individuality, I argue, is a legitimate object of curiosity, especially at the human level, for it is here that we are overwhelmed by this particular natural phenomenon. I venture the opinion that all of the animals in the world are psychologically less distinct from one another than one man is from other men.

There are, of course, many areas of psychology where individuality is of no concern. What is wanted is knowledge about averages, about the generalized human mind, or about types of people. But when we are interested in guiding, or predicting John's behavior, or in understanding the Johnian quality of John, we need to transcend the limitations of a psychology of species, and develop a more adequate psychology of personal growth.

The outlines of the needed psychology of becoming can be discovered by looking within ourselves; for it is knowledge of our own uniqueness that supplies the first, and probably the best, hints for acquiring orderly knowledge of others. True, we should guard against the fallacy of projection: of assuming that other people have states of mind, interests, and values precisely like our own. Yet it is by reflecting upon the factors that seem vital in our own experience of becoming that we identify the issues that are important. When we ask ourselves about our own course of growth such problems as the following come to mind: the nature of our inborn dispositions, the impress of culture and environment upon us, our emerging self-consciousness, our conscience, our gradually evolving style of expression, our experiences of choice and freedom, our handling of conflicts and anxieties, and finally the formation of our maturer values, interests, and aims.

Abraham H. Maslow (1908–)

Toward a Psychology of Health

Perhaps more than any other psychologist, Abraham Maslow deserves the title of founding father of that contemporary movement which seeks a humanistic alternative both to the emasculated scientism of the behaviorists and to the romantic pessimism of the classical Freudians. Among all the diverse currents of thought and research which populate that Third Force, the one for which Maslow is the preeminent spokesman is a "health-and-growth psychology" distinctive in its emphatic affirmation of "full-humanness" and self-actualization, of the constructive possibilities of essential human nature as against its destructive deviations and detours. In a succession of brilliantly creative and provocative theoretical writings, beginning with *Motivation and Personality* (1954), continuing through *Toward a Psychology of Being* (1962), and culminating (to date) in *The Psychology of Science* (1966), Maslow has condemned the traditional preoccupation of psychology with "pessimistic, negative and limited conceptions" of man along with its accompanying neglect of such fully human conditions as love, ecstasy, gaiety, exuberance, the joy of achievement and creativity—in short, the "peak experiences" of mankind. Where psychology in its positivist and Freudian phases "has voluntarily restricted itself to only half of its rightful jurisdiction, and that the darker, meaner half," Maslow has undertaken (as the historians Hall and Lindzey point out)

165

"to supply the other half of the picture, the brighter, better half, and to give a portrait of the whole man."*

In much of his work, most notably *Religions, Values, and Peak-Experiences* (1964) and *New Knowledge in Human Values* (which he edited in 1959), Maslow has been concerned to restore to psychology an appreciation of human values as central both to the nature of man and to his proper study. It is noteworthy that in making this unfashionable case he does not counsel the abandonment of empirical science, despite its rock-ribbed posture of ethical neutrality and general intolerance of all such soft persuasions. Instead he argues (like Teilhard de Chardin) for a broader and deeper empiricism, one capable of comprehending experience along with behavior and of embracing the Within as well as the Without of human life. Science, according to Maslow, "need not abdicate from the problems of love, creativeness, value, beauty, imagination, ethics and joy." Indeed it has shirked these problems in the past, misled by the intolerant dogmas of mechanistic scientism; but "none of this I feel is necessary. All that is needed for science to be a help in positive human fulfillment is an enlarging and deepening of the conception of its nature, its goals and its methods."† In the future construction of such a comprehensive and humane science, in psychology as elsewhere in the study of man, the work of Maslow is likely to play an instrumental part.

The selection which follows is taken from Maslow's *Toward a Psychology of Being.*

THERE IS NOW EMERGING over the horizon a new conception of human sickness and of human health, a psychology that I find so thrilling and so full of wonderful possibilities that

---

*Calvin S. Hall and Gardner Lindzey (eds.), *Theories of Personality* (New York: Wiley, 1957), p. 325.

†Abraham H. Maslow, *Toward a Psychology of Being* (Princeton: Van Nostrand, 1962), p. v.

I yield to the temptation to present it publicly even before it is checked and confirmed, and before it can be called reliable scientific knowledge.

The basic assumptions of this point of view are:

1. We have, each of us, an essential biologically based inner nature, which is to some degree "natural," intrinsic, given, and, in a certain limited sense, unchangeable, or, at least, unchanging.

2. Each person's inner nature is in part unique to himself and in part species-wide.

3. It is possible to study this inner nature scientifically and to discover what it is like—(not *invent—discover*).

4. This inner nature, as much as we know of it so far, seems not to be intrinsically evil, but rather either neutral or positively "good." What we call evil behavior appears most often to be a secondary reaction to frustration of this intrinsic nature.

5. Since this inner nature is good or neutral rather than bad, it is best to bring it out and to encourage it rather than to suppress it. If it is permitted to guide our life, we grow healthy, fruitful, and happy.

6. If this essential core of the person is denied or suppressed, he gets sick sometimes in obvious ways, sometimes in subtle ways, sometimes immediately, sometimes later.

7. This inner nature is not strong and overpowering and unmistakable like the instincts of animals. It is weak and delicate and subtle and easily overcome by habit, cultural pressure, and wrong attitudes toward it.

8. Even though weak, it rarely disappears in the normal person—perhaps not even in the sick person. Even though denied, it persists underground forever pressing for actualization.

9. Somehow, these conclusions must all be articulated with the necessity of discipline, deprivation, frustration, pain, and tragedy. To the extent that these experiences reveal and foster and fulfill our inner nature, to that extent they are desirable experiences.

Observe that if these assumptions are proven true, they promise a scientific ethics, a natural value system, a court of ultimate appeal for the determination of good and bad, of right and wrong. The more we learn about man's natural tendencies, the easier it will be to tell him how to be good, how to be happy, how to be fruitful, how to respect himself, how to love, how to fulfill his highest potentialities. This amounts to automatic solution of many of the personality problems of the future. The thing to do seems to be to find out what *you* are *really* like inside, deep down, as a member of the human species and as a particular individual.

The study of such healthy people can teach us much about our own mistakes, our shortcomings, the proper directions in which to grow. Every age but ours has had its model, its ideal. All of these have been given up by our culture; the saint, the hero, the gentleman, the knight, the mystic. About all we have left is the well-adjusted man without problems, a very pale and doubtful substitute. Perhaps we shall soon be able to use as our guide and model the fully growing and self-fulfilling human being, the one in whom all his potentialities are coming to full development, the one whose inner nature expresses itself freely, rather than being warped, suppressed, or denied.

The serious thing for each person to recognize vividly and poignantly, each for himself, is that every falling away from species-virtue, every crime against one's own nature, every evil act, *every one without exception records itself* in our unconscious and makes us despise ourselves. Karen Horney had a good word to describe this unconscious perceiving and remembering; she said it "registers." If we do something we are ashamed of, it "registers" to our discredit, and if we do something honest or fine or good, it "registers" to our credit. The net results ultimately are either one or the other—either we respect and accept ourselves or we despise ourselves and feel contemptible, worthless, and unlovable. Theologians used to use the word "*accidie*" to describe the sin of failing to do with one's life all that one knows one could do.

This point of view in no way denies the usual Freudian picture. But it does add to it and supplement it. To oversimplify the matter somewhat, it is as if Freud supplied to us the sick half of psychology and we must now fill it out with the healthy half. Perhaps this health psychology will give us more possibility for controlling and improving our lives and for making ourselves better people. Perhaps this will be more fruitful than asking "how to get *unsick*."

How can we encourage free development? What are the best educational conditions for it? Sexual? Economic? Political? What kind of world do we need for such people to grow in? What kind of world will such people create? Sick people are made by a sick culture; healthy people are made possible by a healthy culture. But it is just as true that sick individuals make their culture more sick and that healthy individuals make their culture more healthy. Improving individual health is one approach to making a better world. To express it in another way, encouragement of personal growth is a real possibility; cure of actual neurotic symptoms is far less possible without outside help. It is relatively easy to try deliberately to make oneself a more honest man; it is very difficult to try to cure one's own compulsions or obsessions.

The classical approach to personality problems considers

them to be problems in an undesirable sense. Struggle, conflict, guilt, bad conscience, anxiety, depression, frustration, tension, shame, self-punishment, feeling of inferiority or unworthiness—they all cause psychic pain, they disturb efficiency of performance, and they are uncontrollable. They are therefore automatically regarded as sick and undesirable and they get "cured" away as soon as possible.

But all of these symptoms are found also in healthy people, or in people who are growing toward health. Supposing you *should* feel guilty and don't? Supposing you have attained a nice stabilization of forces and you *are* adjusted? Perhaps adjustment and stabilization, while good because it cuts your pain, is also bad because development toward a higher ideal ceases?

Erich Fromm, in a very important book, attacked the classical Freudian notion of a superego because this concept was entirely authoritarian and relativistic. That is to say, your superego or your conscience was supposed by Freud to be primarily the internalization of the wishes, demands, and ideals of the father and mother, whoever they happen to be. But supposing they are criminals? Then what kind of conscience do you have? Or supposing you have a rigid moralizing father who hates fun? Or a psychopath? This conscience exists—Freud was right. We do get our ideals largely from such early figures and not from Sunday School books read later in life. But there is also another element in conscience, or, if you like, another kind of conscience which we all have either weakly or strongly. And this is the "intrinsic conscience." This is based upon the unconscious and preconscious perception of our own nature, of our own destiny, of our own capacities, of our own "call" in life. It insists that we be true to our inner nature and that we do not deny it out of weakness or for advantage or for any other reason. He who belies his talent, the born painter who sells stockings instead, the intelligent man who lives a stupid life, the man who sees the truth and keeps his mouth shut, the coward who gives up his manliness, all these people perceive in a deep way that they have done wrong to themselves and despise themselves for it. Out of this self-punishment may come only neurosis, but there may equally well come renewed courage, righteous indignation, increased self-respect, because of thereafter doing the right thing; in a word, growth and improvement can come through pain and conflict.

In essence I am deliberately rejecting our present easy distinction between sickness and health, at least as far as surface symptoms are concerned. Does sickness mean having symptoms? I maintain now that sickness might consist of *not* having symptoms when you should. Does health mean being symptom-free? I deny it. Which of the Nazis at Auschwitz or Dachau were healthy? Those with stricken conscience or those with a nice, clear, happy conscience? Was it possible for a profoundly human person not to feel conflict, suffering, depression, rage, etc?

In a word if you tell me you have a personality problem I am not certain until I know you better whether to say "Good!" or "I'm sorry." It depends on the reasons. And these, it seems, may be bad reasons, or they may be good reasons.

An example is the changing attitude of psychologists toward popularity, toward adjustment, even toward delinquency. Popular with whom? Perhaps it is better for a youngster to be *unpopular* with the neighboring snobs or with the local country club set. Adjusted to what? To a bad culture? To a dominating parent? What shall we think of a well-adjusted slave? A well-adjusted prisoner? Even the behavior problem boy is being looked upon with new tolerance. *Why* is he delinquent? Most often it is for sick reasons. But occasionally it is for good reasons and the boy is simply resisting exploitation, domination, neglect, contempt, and trampling upon.

Clearly what will be called personality problems depends on who is doing the calling. The slave owner? The dictator? The patriarchal father? The husband who wants his wife to remain a child? It seems quite clear that personality problems may sometimes be loud protests against the crushing of one's psychological bones, of one's true inner nature. What is sick then is *not* to protest while this crime is being committed. And I am sorry to report my impression that most people do not protest under such treatment. They take it and pay years later, in neurotic and psychosomatic symptoms of various kinds, or perhaps in some cases never become aware that they are sick, that they have missed true happiness, true fulfillment of promise, a rich emotional life, and a serene, fruitful old age, that they have never known how wonderful it is to be creative, to react aesthetically, to find life thrilling.

The question of desirable grief and pain or the necessity for it must also be faced. Is growth and self-fulfillment possible at all without pain and grief and sorrow and turmoil? If these are to some extent necessary and unavoidable, then to what extent? If grief and pain are sometimes necessary for growth of the person, then we must learn not to protect people from them automatically as if they were always bad. Sometimes they may be good and desirable in view of the ultimate good consequences. Not allowing people to go through their pain, and protecting them from it, may turn out to be a kind of overprotection, which in turn implies a certain lack of respect for the integrity and the intrinsic nature and the future development of the individual.

PART IV

Helpers and Healers:

Psychiatry, Psychoanalysis, Psychotherapy

Philippe Pinel (1745–1826)

A Treatise on Insanity

"During the eighteenth century," observed the great psychiatrist Emil Kraepelin a hundred years later, "the plight of the mentally ill was shocking almost everywhere in Europe." Despised and feared, the so-called insane were nowhere understood and rarely attended to in a medical manner; instead they were regarded as wild animals bereft not merely of "sense" but of all humanity, for whom chains were an elementary precaution and the cruelest punishments a salutary form of treatment. But the century of enlightenment also brought the first significant steps toward humanitarian reform and scientific rehabilitation. "The latter part of the eighteenth century," as Walter Bromberg points out in his history of psychotherapy, *The Mind of Man*, "was the nodal point at which the forces of humanitarianism and political emancipation met the bankruptcy of medical science to heal the mentally distraught. . . . It was the nodal point that turned the tide against misidentifying the insane with evil and identifying them with humanity."*

The new spirit was displayed almost simultaneously during the last decade of the century in England, with the founding of the York Retreat by the farsighted Quaker, William Tuke; in Italy, where Vincenzio Chiarugi freed the insane of Florence from their chains; and in France,

---

*Walter Bromberg, *The Mind of Man: A History of Psychotherapy and Psychoanalysis* (New York: Harper Torchbooks, 1959), p. 82.

where Pinel dared to carry the ideals of 1789 into the lunatic asylum of the Bicêtre. Following his appointment as asylum physician in 1793, Pinel confronted the tough prison-commission member of the Paris Commune, Couthon, with his proposal to liberate the fettered victims of insanity. "Why not," replied the old warden, "proceed to the zoo and liberate the lions and tigers?" However, with what must have been extraordinary persuasiveness, Pinel finally prevailed; and they entered the buildings in which some three hundred "maniacs" met them with screams and the clanking of chains. "Citizen," exclaimed Couthon in horror, "are you not yourself mad that you would free these beasts?" To which Pinel responded: "I am convinced that these *people* are not incurable if they can have air and liberty." He then moved among the inmates, releasing some from stone posts to which they were chained by the ankle, talking to others, giving sympathetic attention to all. One of those he liberated, a former soldier confined in the asylum for a decade, later saved his life when a mob of revolutionary citizens was about to lynch him under the delusion that the asylum was harboring enemies of the people.

With respect to his experiment in emancipation, Pinel wrote in the preface to his major work, the *Treatise on Insanity*: "I have examined with scrupulous care the effects which the iron chains had on the insane, and afterward the comparative results of their removal, and I cannot help favoring a wiser and more moderate restraint."* In addition to the removal of fetters, Pinel inaugurated a system of treatment which abandoned the time-honored devices of bloodletting, flogging, ducking, purging, and general torture of the mentally disturbed. Two years later, in 1795, he was placed in charge of La Salpêtrière, a less backward institution where Pinel was enabled to carry out his entire program of reform and rehabilitation, and in so doing to advance the sciences of psychotherapy and psychiatry. "The great

---

*Philippe Pinel, *Traité Medico-Philosophique sur l'Aliénation Mentale* (1809), quoted in A. A. Roback, *History of Psychology and Psychiatry* (New York: Philosophical Library, 1961), p. 270.

contribution of Pinel and his followers," according to Bromberg, "was the recognition that an insane person was not
another kind of being, but simply a human being with
an illness, with which physicians, without loss of dignity,
could grapple."*

NOTHING HAS MORE CONTRIBUTED to the rapid improvement
of modern natural history, than the spirit of minute and
accurate observation which has distinguished its votaries.
The habit of analytical investigation, thus adopted, has
induced an accuracy of expression and a propriety of classification, which have themselves, in no small degree, contributed to the advancement of natural knowledge. Convinced
of the essential importance of the same means in the illustration of a subject so new and difficult as that of the present
work, it will be seen that I have availed myself of their application, in all or most of the instances of this most calami-
tous disease, which occurred in my practice at the Asylum
de Bicêtre. On my entrance upon the duties of that hospital,
every thing presented to me the appearance of chaos and
confusion. Some of my unfortunate patients laboured under
the horrors of a most gloomy and desponding melancholy.
Others were furious, and subject to the influence of a per-
petual delirium. Some appeared to possess a correct judge-
ment upon most subjects, but were occasionally agitated by
violent sallies of maniacal fury; while those of another class
were sunk into a state of stupid idiotism and imbecility.
Symptoms so different, and all comprehended under the
general title of insanity, required, on my part, much study
and discrimination; and to secure order in the establishment
and success to the practice, I determined upon adopting such

---

*Bromberg, *op. cit.*, p. 84.

a variety of measures, both as to discipline and treatment, as my patient required, and my limited opportunity permitted. From systems of nosology, I had little assistance to expect; since the arbitrary distribution of Sauvages and Cullen were better calculated to impress the conviction of their insufficiency than to simplify my labour. I, therefore, resolved to adopt that method of investigation which has invariably succeeded in all the departments of natural history, viz, to notice successively every fact, without any other object than that of collecting materials for future use; and to endeavour, as far as possible, to divest myself of the influence, both of my own prepossessions and the authority of others. With this view, I first of all took a general statement of the symptoms of my patients. To ascertain their characteristic peculiarities, the above survey was followed by cautious and repeated examinations into the condition of individuals. All our new cases were entered at great length upon the journals of the house. Due attention was paid to the changes of the seasons and the weather, and their respective influences upon the patients were minutely noticed. Having a peculiar attachment for the more general method of descriptive history, I did not confine myself to any exclusive mode of arranging my observations, nor to any one system of nosography. The facts which I have thus collected are now submitted to the consideration of the public, in the form of a regular treatise.

All civilised nations, however different in their customs, and manner of living, will never fail to have some causes of insanity in common; and, it is natural to believe, that all will do their utmost to remedy the evil. Why may not France, as well as England, adopt the means, from the use of which, no nation is by nature proscribed, and which are alone discovered by observation and experience? But success, in this

department of medical enquiry, must depend upon the con-
currence of many favourable circumstances. The loss of a
friend, who became insane through excessive love of glory,
in 1783, and the inaptitude of pharmaceutic preparations to
a mind elated, as his was, with a high sense of its independence, enhanced my admiration of the judicious precepts of
the ancients, and made me regret that I had it not then in
my power to put them in practice.

About that time I was engaged to attend, in a professional
capacity, at an asylum, where I made observations upon this
disease for five successive years. My opportunities for the application of moral remedies, were, however, not numerous.
Having no part of the management of the interior police of
that institution, I had little or no influence over its servants.
The person who was at the head of the establishment, had
no interest in the cure of his wealthy patients, and he often,
unequivocally, betrayed a desire, that every remedy should
fail. At other times, he placed exclusive confidence in the
utility of bathing, or in the efficacy of petty and frivolous
recipes. The administration of the civil hospitals, in Paris,
opened to me in the second year of the republic a wide field
of research, by my nomination to the office of chief physician
to the national Asylum de Bicêtre, which I continued to fill
for two years. In order, in some degree, to make up for the
local disadvantages of the hospital, and the numerous incon-
veniences which arose from the instability and successive
changes of the administration, I determined to turn my
attention, almost exclusively, to the subject of moral treatment. The halls and the passages of the hospital were much
confined, and so arranged as to render the cold of winter
and the heat of summer equally intolerable and injurious.
The chambers were exceedingly small and inconvenient.
Baths we had none, though I made repeated applications

for them; nor had we extensive liberties for walking, gardening or other exercises. So destitute of accommodations, we found it impossible to class our patients according to the varieties and degrees of their respective maladies. On the other hand, the gentleman, to whom was committed the chief management of the hospital, exercised towards all that were placed under his protection, the vigilance of a kind and affectionate parent. Accustomed to reflect, and possessed of great experience, he was not deficient either in the knowledge or execution of the duties of his office. He never lost sight of the principles of a most genuine philanthropy. He paid great attention to the diet of the house, and left no opportunity for murmur or discontent on the part of the most fastidious. He exercised a strict discipline over the conduct of the domestics, and punished, with severity, every instance of ill treatment, and every act of violence, of which they were guilty towards those whom it was merely their duty to serve. He was both esteemed and feared by every maniac; for he was mild, and at the same time inflexibly firm. In a word, he was master of every branch of his art, from its simplest to its most complicated principles. Thus was I introduced to a man, whose friendship was an invaluable acquisition to me. Our acquaintance matured into the closest intimacy. Our duties and inclinations concurred in the same object. Our conversation, which was almost exclusively professional, contributed to our mutual improvement. With those advantages, I devoted a great part of my time in examining for myself the various and numerous affections of the human mind in a state of disease. I regularly took notes of whatever appeared deserving of my attention; and compared what I thus collected, with facts analogous to them that I met with in books, or amongst my own memoranda of former dates. Such are the materials upon which my principles of moral treatment are founded.

Emil Kraepelin (1855–1926)

Early Treatment of the Mentally Ill

It was Kraepelin, at the end of the nineteenth century, who first systematically classified the knowledge and concepts of the growing branch of psychiatry which dealt with the psychoses. His painstaking experimental and descriptive methods owed much to a ten-year discipleship under Wundt at Leipzig, after which he applied the Wundtian methods for the first time to the problems of psychopathology. His own psychiatric clinic at the University of Heidelberg became famous for the range and rigor of its research projects. "General psychology is beholden to Kraepelin in no small measure," according to Roback; "for his laboratory was organized as no other in this field, with specific problems assigned to graduate students and assistants. There were investigations on the depth of sleep, ergographical studies, experiments on expectation, surprise, and disappointment."[*]

His principal contribution, however, remains the comprehensive ordering of psychiatric nosology into a system which with minor variations still prevails today. On the basis of the "life-history" schema, Kraepelin brought together the hitherto unrelated symptoms of illness into meaningful perspectives and patterns. Although he did not make most of the discoveries himself, his ideas of manic-

---

[*]A. A. Roback, *History of Psychology and Psychiatry* (New York: Philosophical Library, 1961), p. 308.

depression, dementia praecox, and the effect of drugs upon personality disturbance, climaxed the work of a generation of European pioneers and laid the foundation for modern clinical psychiatry.

The selection which follows is taken from Kraepelin: *One Hundred Years of Psychiatry*.

DURING THE EIGHTEENTH CENTURY the plight of the mentally ill was shocking almost everywhere in Europe. We know that they were generally handled like idlers, vagrants and criminals; the punitive laws to which they were subjected were rarely administered humanely. Some were allowed through the benevolence of their fellow men to eke out a penurious existence as beggars or harmless lunatics. Flighty, troublesome or dangerous patients were restrained and kept in a small room or stall in a private house, in "lunatic boxes," in cages or in other places of confinement that seemed appropriate for isolating them and rendering them harmless. Only a few of them were admitted to hospitals, such as the Juliusspital in Würzburg, where they could receive special attention and medical care. As a result of poor supervision, many committed suicide, perished through accidents or created serious disturbances. The tense and exasperating environment thus created encouraged the establishment of the strictest preventive measures.

There were in Germany at that time no special institutions for the insane but only wards in poorhouses, prisons, orphanages, workhouses and hospitals in which troublesome mental patients were confined. "We lock these unfortunate creatures in lunatic cells, as if they were criminals," exclaimed Reil in 1803, "We keep them in chains in forlorn jails, near the roosts of owls in hidden recesses above the gates of towns, or in the damp cellars of reformatories where no sympathetic human being can ever bestow on them a friendly glance, and we let them rot in their own filth. Their fetters scrape the flesh from their bones, and their wan, hollow faces search for the grave that their wailing and our ignominy conceals from them." Writers of that time never tired of setting down terrifying descriptions of the insane and their surroundings. One anonymous reporter wrote in 1795: "A humanitarian is bound to shudder when he discovers the plight of the unfortunate victims of this dreadful affliction; many of them grovel in their own filth on unclean straw that is seldom changed, often stark naked and in chains, in dark, damp dungeons where no breath of fresh air can enter. Under such terrifying conditions, it would be easier for the most rational person to become insane than for a madman to regain his sanity." He added that in one so-called asylum which he visted, five out of nine died during the summer. In 1818 Esquirol in Paris wrote in the same vein to the minister of the interior: "I saw patients naked, with rags or nothing more than straw to protect them against the cold, damp weather. I saw how in their wretched state they were deprived of fresh air to breathe, of water to quench their thirst, and of the basic necessities of life. I saw them turned over for safekeeping to brutal jailors. I saw them chained in damp, cramped holes without light or air; people would be ashamed to keep in such places the wild animals which are cared for at great expense in our large cities. That is what I observed almost everywhere in France, and that is how the mentally ill are treated almost everywhere in Europe."

"It is indeed frightening," explained Frank in 1804, "to approach such a wretched and sorrowful place! To hear mingled shouts of exultation and despair and then to think

that within are human beings once renowned for their talent
and sensitivity. It is terrifying to go inside and be assailed
by these filthy, ragged creatures, while others are prevented
from joining in the assault only by their fetters and chains
or by the jabs of their attendants." In the same year Hoch
reported: "In the asylum in Berlin those who are stark raving
mad are isolated for the duration of their madness; they are
locked naked in small cages or hutches, and food and water
are introduced through holes and placed in copper basins
secured by chains." He recommended that asylums be established in remote, isolated places since the wailing and
howling of deranged patients disturbed all sane men and
upset the whole community. Stupid or mentally deficient
patients, because they seemed passively to endure whatever
was inflicted upon them, gave rise to the popular assumption
(rejected by Tuke) that they were insensitive to hunger,
cold, and pain even though the opposite was proven by their
obvious emaciation, by their frozen members, and by their
dying from injuries. The result was that their suffering was
looked upon as self-evident and unalterable while the significance of their plight was never fully appreciated.

The conditions just described persisted until well along
in the nineteenth century. In 1842 an investigation of housing conditions in Holland revealed patients "lying naked on
filthy straw in foul air, frequently in chains, under a blanket;
many were without sufficient food; men and women were in-
discriminately mingled, and to all appearances some of them
had not seen daylight for a long time." But in 1843 Mahir
described the present-day Narrenturm in Vienna (a circular
five-story building with room in its 139 cells for between
200 and 250 mental patients) in these words: "The dark
cells and corridors, secured by massive iron doors and gates
and by awesome chains and locks, strongly suggest its prison-

like character; to escape from it would defy the efforts of the most accomplished criminal or miscreant. The doctors who visit this dungeon are greeted by its inordinate filth, by its abominable, unbearable stench, noise and howling, and by the terrifying, heart-rending cries of many lunatics whose arms and legs—or even necks—are cruelly shackled in heavy chains and iron rings. I have seen many wretched mental patients, but the most wretched of all were those who had been caged and treated like wild beasts. Not even the worst menagerie would exhibit such unfriendly, inhumane conditions. The faces and actions of the lunatics revealed their intense pain, suffering and despair. Their meager fare and their unending physical suffering, aggravated by the senseless application of vesicants and pustulants, made their plight worse than that of even the most vicious criminals and murderers, for these piteous creatures never saw a ray of sunshine nor the full light of day. A tiny hole guarded by a heavy iron grill was the only opening through which diagnosis and treatment could be accomplished. The attending physician was greeted by weeping and wailing, by insults and imprecations. Through the same hole brutal, unsympathetic wardens pushed food and drink for the much abused madmen, as if they were wolves and hyenas."

Chains were commonly used a hundred years ago to shackle patients to the wall or to rings in the floor. Physicians then entertained an unwarranted fear of lunatics, as laymen still do, and ascribed to them extraordinary physical strength because of their rash conduct. No effort was spared to render them harmless. On his official visit to Juliusspital in 1700 Müller found in the middle of each ward for mental patients a huge stone post with chains suitable for subduing and "disciplining restless or troublesome patients." Hayner also noted that in Waldheim it was not until 1807 that he managed to abolish "the abominable use" of chains. Conolly alleged that in a large private institution in England 70 out of 400 patients were kept in chains almost continuously for a period of twenty years.

Those who visited Bedlam in London in 1814 could see countless patients clad only in loose shrouds and chained by their arms or legs to the wall in such a way that they could stand upright or remain seated. One patient for twelve years wore rings around his neck and waist and was tethered to a wall; because he had resisted attempts to control his movements by means of a chain manipulated from a neighboring room, the warden had also taken the precaution of lashing his arms to his sides. An administrator explained that chains were the surest device for restraining recalcitrant mental patients. Even Dr. Monro stated in response to an investigating committee of the House of Commons that no one dared use chains on noblemen, but that they were indispensable in dealing with the poor and with those in public institutions. Güntz in his travels noted that in 1853 in Gheel (Belgium) fetters and chains were still in use.

Rivaling chains in popularity was the lash. Müller related that in the Juliusspital attendants were generously provided with many restraining and punitive devices—chains, manacles, shackles, and efficient, leather-encased bullwhips. They made ample use of these instruments whenever a patient complained, littered his quarters, or became recalcitrant or abusive. "Thrashing was almost a part of the daily routine," he concluded. Lichtenberg explained that thrashings were often better for lunatics than anything else, and that they helped them to adjust to the harsh realities of daily life. Even Reil, the enthusiastic champion of mental care for the insane, noted that the strait jacket, confinement, hunger, and a few lashes with the bullwhip would readily bring patients into line.

Frank was also of the opinion that "a light blow" was "effective in dealing with malicious or unreasonable patients." Autenrieth found that women who persisted in going around naked quickly dressed in response to a few applications of the lash. Neumann recommended the lash for uncleanliness. He said that it was generally effective, especially when benevolently applied. Langermann, the highly esteemed reformer who worked with Prussian mental patients, wrote as late as 1804 that doctors should when necessary resort to imprisonment, punishment, and flogging. Hayner in 1817 spoke out vehemently against physical chastisement of the insane, calling it unjustified, shameful, and unnecessary. "From this day on," he exclaimed, "let no one strike a single victim from the piteous ranks of these patients! I curse any man, great or small, who sanctions the beating of a man devoid of understanding!"

Sigmund Freud   (1856–1939)

The Theory of Instincts

The most influential figure in the history of psychology,
and one of the half-dozen most influential figures in the
entire history of thought, Sigmund Freud was the leader
of a revolution in the mental sciences which is still being
fought out a generation after his death. Ironically, the
greatest psychologist of them all brought to his calling
virtually no formal training in psychology and little more
reading acquaintance; his entire background was in the
physical sciences and their medical applications. "It would
appear that in his approach to the mind, lacking a key to
the conventional front door of consciousness, Freud had no
choice but to enter through the basement—with all its
darkly impressive tangle of power machinery, naked pipe-
lines and seething cauldrons."* In view of the strong
mechanistic bias of his background and early writing, it is
remarkable that Freud did not follow the route of experimental psychology and end up in the camp of conditioned-
reflex therapy; instead he struck out in the opposite direction and founded a system of psychoanalysis premised upon
the independent reality of mind—and, more heretically
still, of *unconscious* mind. Freud was not alone in daring
to challenge the reigning shibboleths of academic psychology
(and of organic medicine) at the turn of the century; but

---

*Floyd W. Matson, *The Broken Image: Man, Science and Society* (New York:
Braziller, 1964), p. 196.

he was without peer or precedent in the success with which he carried the attack and won ultimate acceptance for the basic tenets of his system of psychological theory and therapy.

Freud's theory of instincts, of the contents or levels of the human mind, was successively refined and modified (and at least once drastically altered) from its first formulation in 1900 until his death in 1939. His last testimony on the subject was contained in the posthumously published *Outline of Psychoanalysis*, from which the present selection has been taken. One of the most significant later additions to Freud's "topographical" layout of the mind was the hypothesis of a "death instinct" (*Thanatos*), independent of the "life instinct" (*Eros*) which earlier had been thought to rule the primal state of human nature unopposed. Indeed, to Freud in the pessimistic mood of his later years— as expressed in such meta-psychological writings as *Civilization and Its Discontents, The Future of an Illusion*, and an exchange of letters with Einstein on war and peace ("Why War?")*—human existence was a constant struggle between man-as-instinct and his repressive civilization, and on another level between the forces of life and death within each individual. This brooding apprehension of original sin, of intrinsic evil in the heart of man, gave Freud the appearance of an Old Testament prophet armed with modern scholarship; and in recent years it has brought him renewed attention from a generation obsessed with the contingent possibilities of nuclear extermination. "Freud was right," maintains Norman O. Brown, "in positing a death instinct, and the development of nuclear weapons of destruction makes our present dilemma plain: we either come to terms with our unconscious instincts and drives—with life and with death—or else we surely die."†

---

*For the correspondence with Einstein, see the *Collected Papers of Sigmund Freud* (New York: International Psychoanalytic Press, Vol. V, 1950), pp. 273–287.

†Norman O. Brown, *Life Against Death* (Middletown: Wesleyan University Press, 1959), p. x.

THE POWER OF THE id expresses the true purpose of the individual organism's life. This consists in the satisfaction of its innate needs. No such purpose as that of keeping itself alive or of protecting itself from dangers by means of anxiety can be attributed to the id. That is the business of the ego, which is also concerned with discovering the most favorable and least perilous method of obtaining satisfaction, taking the external world into account. The superego may bring fresh needs to the fore, but its chief function remains the *limitation* of satisfactions.

The forces which we assume to exist behind the tensions caused by the needs of the id are called *instincts*. They represent the somatic demands upon mental life. Though they are the ultimate cause of all activity, they are by nature conservative; the state, whatever it may be, which a living thing has reached, gives rise to a tendency to re-establish that state so soon as it has been abandoned. It is possible to distinguish an indeterminate number of instincts and in common practice this is in fact done. For us, however, the important question arises whether we may not be able to derive all of these instincts from a few fundamental ones. We have found that instincts can change their aim (by displacement) and also that they can replace one another—the energy of one instinct passing over to another. This latter process is still insufficiently understood. After long doubts and vacillations we have decided to assume the existence of only two basic instincts, *Eros* and *the destructive instinct*. (The contrast between the instincts of self-preservation and of the preservation of the species, as well as the contrast between ego-love and object-love, fall within the bounds of Eros.) The aim of the first of these basic instincts is to establish

ever greater unities and to preserve them thus—in short, to
bind together; the aim of the second, on the contrary, is to
undo connections and so to destroy things. We may suppose
that the final aim of the destructive instinct is to reduce
living things to an inorganic state. For this reason we also
call it the *death instinct*. If we suppose that living things
appeared later than inanimate ones and arose out of them,
then the death instinct agrees with the formula that we have
stated, to the effect that instincts tend toward a return to an
earlier state. We are unable to apply the formula to Eros
(the love instinct). That would be to imply that living
substance had once been a unity but had subsequently been
torn apart and was now tending toward re-union.[1]

In biological functions the two basic instincts work against
each other or combine with each other. Thus, the act of
eating is a destruction of the object with the final aim of
incorporating it, and the sexual act is an act of aggression
having as its purpose the most intimate union. This interaction of the two basic instincts with and against each other
gives rise to the whole variegation of the phenomena of life.
The analogy of our two basic instincts extends from the region of animate things to the pair of opposing forces—attrac-
tion and repulsion—which rule in the inorganic world.[2]

Modifications in the proportions of the fusion between the
instincts have the most noticeable results. A surplus of sexual
aggressiveness will change a lover into a sexual murderer,
while a sharp diminution in the aggressive factor will lead
to shyness or impotence.

There can be no question of restricting one or the other
of the basic instincts to a single region of the mind. They
are necessarily present everywhere. We may picture an
initial state of things by supposing that the whole available
energy of Eros, to which we shall henceforward give the

name of *libido,* is present in the as yet undifferentiated ego-id and serves to neutralize the destructive impulses which are simultaneously present. (There is no term analogous to "libido" for describing the energy of the destructive instinct.) It becomes relatively easy for us to follow the later vicissitudes of the libido; but this is more difficult with the destructive instinct.

So long as that instinct operates internally, as a death instinct, it remains silent; we only come across it after it has become diverted outward as an instinct of destruction. That that diversion should occur seems essential for the preservation of the individual; the musculature is employed for the purpose. When the superego begins to be formed, considerable amounts of the aggressive instinct become fixated within the ego and operate there in a self-destructive fashion. This is one of the dangers to health to which mankind become subject on the path to cultural development. The holding back of aggressiveness is in general unhealthy and leads to illness. A person in a fit of rage often demonstrates how the transition from restrained aggressiveness to self-destructiveness is effected, by turning his aggressiveness against himself: he tears his hair or beats his face with his fists—treatment which he would evidently have preferred to apply to someone else. Some portion of self-destructiveness remains permanently within, until it at length succeeds in doing the individual to death, not, perhaps, until his libido has been used up or has become fixated in some disadvantageous way. Thus it may in general be suspected that the *individual* dies of his internal conflicts but that the *species* dies of its unsuccessful struggle against the external world, when the latter undergoes changes of a kind that cannot be dealt with by the adaptations which the species has acquired.

It is difficult to say anything of the behavior of the libido in the id and in the superego. Everything that we know about it relates to the ego, in which the whole available amount of libido is at first stored up. We call this state of things absolute, primary *narcissism*. It continues until the ego begins to cathect the presentations of objects with libido—to change narcissistic libido into *object libido*. Throughout life the ego remains the great reservoir from which libidinal cathexes[3] are sent out on to objects and into which they are also once more withdrawn, like the pseudopodia of a body of protoplasm. It is only when someone is completely in love that the main quantity of libido is transferred on to the object and the object to some extent takes the place of the ego. A characteristic of libido which is important in life is its *mobility*, the ease with which it passes from one object to another. This must be contrasted with the *fixation* of libido to particular objects, which often persists through life.

There can be no question that the libido has somatic sources, that it streams into the ego from various organs and parts of the body. This is most clearly seen in the case of the portion of the libido which, from its instinctual aim, is known as sexual excitation. The most prominent of the parts of the body from which this libido arises are described by the name of *erotogenic zones*, though strictly speaking the whole body is an erotogenic zone. The greater part of what we know about Eros—that is, about its exponent, the libido—has been gained from the study of the sexual function, which, indeed, in the popular view, if not in our theory, coincides with Eros. We have been able to form a picture of the way in which the sexual impulse, which is destined to exercise a decisive influence on our life, gradually develops out of successive contributions from a number of component instincts, which represent particular erotogenic zones.

NOTES

[1]Something of the sort has been imagined by poets, but nothing like it is known to us from the actual history of living substance.

[2]This picture of the basic forces or instincts, which still arouses much opposition among analysts, was already a familiar one to the philosopher Empedocles of Acragas.

[3][The words "cathexis" and "to cathect" are used as renderings of the German *"Besetzung"* and *"besetzen."* These are the terms with which Freud expresses the idea of psychical energy being lodged in or attaching itself to mental structures or processes, somewhat on the analogy of an electric charge.—*Trans.*]

Carl Gustav Jung   (1875–1961)

The Undiscovered Self

In the first years of its insurgency, coinciding with the opening decade of the twentieth century, the psychoanalytic
movement took the form of a closed Vienna circle with
Freud at its center ringed around by a handful of disciples.
Partly because of the embattled character of the movement
(as psychology, as medicine, and as science), partly because
of the authoritarian personality of its founding father, and
for various other reasons, the Freudian school was wracked
by violent quarrels and schisms during the decades that
followed. One by one the principal leaders—the "old Bolshe-
viks" of the movement—fell into deviationist heresies and
were cast out: first Alfred Adler, then Carl Jung and Wilhelm Stekel (both in the same year of 1912), later Otto
Rank, and last of all Sandor Ferenczi. Each defection, of
course, had its peculiar history and pathology; but it is
noteworthy that all of those who dared to disagree with
Freud did so at least in part on the basis of dissatisfaction
with his scientistic reduction of experience and behavior to
past events in general and to sexual etiology in particular.
There was also a common discontent with the mechanistic-
materialist bias in Freudian theory, and with its implications for the relationship of therapist and patient. In
keeping with the canons of scientific objectivity, Freud
counseled a posture of thorough detachment on the part

of the physician—who was to remain a "blank screen" and at all costs to avoid the pitfalls of countertransference.

No one more persistently opposed these emphases of the orthodox Freudian school than Carl Gustav Jung, the Swiss psychoanalyst who came to formulate his own separate system of thought and therapy centered upon the concept of "individuation" or integration of the personality. As against Freud's stress upon past conflicts and drives, Jung asserted that "the mind lives by aims" as well. He was less concerned with scientific analysis of the patient's trouble than with his prospective *synthesis*, expressed in terms of wholeness and dynamic organization of the personality. This emphasis upon individuality and creative potential, upon self-realization and "becoming," led Jung during an unusually long career to place ever greater reliance upon the therapeutic objective of *understanding* the patient in his unique particularity, as opposed to the conventional tasks of classification and diagnosis of symptoms. Toward the end of his life, in a small but significant book entitled *The Undiscovered Self*, Jung entered a passionate plea for a conception of the practice of psychoanalysis as a "whole-souled" encounter in which the resources of both partners are fully and openly engaged, without artificial role-playing or defensive disguises. In this "dialogical" approach to the therapeutic relationship, Jung may be seen to have been saying much the same counter-Freudian things as the existentialist school of psychoanalysis in Europe and the client-centered school of psychotherapy led by Carl R. Rogers in America.

IN THIS BROAD BELT of unconsciousness, which is immune to conscious criticism and control, we stand defenseless, open to all kinds of influences and psychic infections. As with all dangers, we can guard against the risk of psychic infection only when we know what is attacking us, and how, where and when the attack will come. Since self-knowledge is a matter of getting to know the individual facts, theories help very little in this respect. For the more a theory lays claim to universal validity, the less capable it is of doing justice to the individual facts. Any theory based on experience is necessarily *statistical*; that is to say, it formulates an *ideal average* which abolishes all exceptions at either end of the scale and replaces them by an abstract mean. This mean is quite valid, though it need not necessarily occur in reality. Despite this it figures in the theory as an unassailable fundamental fact. The exceptions at either extreme, though equally factual, do not appear in the final result at all, since they cancel each other out. If, for instance, I determine the weight of each stone in a bed of pebbles and get an average weight of 145 grams, this tells me very little about the real nature of the pebbles. Anyone who thought, on the basis of these findings, that he could pick up a pebble of 145 grams at the first try would be in for a serious disappointment. Indeed, it might well happen that however long he searched he would not find a single pebble weighing exactly 145 grams.

The statistical method shows the facts in the light of the ideal average but does not give us a picture of their empirical reality. While reflecting an indisputable aspect of reality, it can falsify the actual truth in a most misleading way. This is particularly true of theories which are based on statistics. The distinctive thing about real facts, however, is their individuality. Not to put too fine a point on it, one could say that the real picture consists of nothing but exceptions to the rule, and that, in consequence, absolute reality has predominantly the character of *irregularity*.

These considerations must be borne in mind whenever there is talk of a theory serving as a guide to self-knowledge. There is and can be no self-knowledge based on theoretical assumptions, for the object of self-knowledge is an individual—a relative exception and an irregular phenomenon.

Hence it is not the universal and the regular that characterize the individual, but rather the unique. He is not to be understood as a recurrent unit but as something unique and singular which in the last analysis can neither be known nor compared with anything else. At the same time man, as member of a species, can and must be described as a statistical unit; otherwise nothing general could be said about him. For this purpose he has to be regarded as a comparative unit. This results in a universally valid anthropology or psychology, as the case may be, with an abstract picture of man as an average unit from which all individual features have been removed. But it is precisely these features which are of paramount importance for *understanding* man. If I want to understand an individual human being, I must lay aside all scientific knowledge of the average man and discard all theories in order to adopt a completely new and unprejudiced attitude. I can only approach the task of *understanding* with a free and open mind, whereas *knowledge* of man, or insight into human character, presupposes all sorts of knowledge about mankind in general.

Now whether it is a question of understanding a fellow human being or of self-knowledge, I must in both cases leave all theoretical assumptions behind me. Since scientific knowledge not only enjoys universal esteem but, in the eyes of modern man, counts as the only intellectual and spiritual authority, understanding the individual obliges me to commit *lèse majesté*, so to speak, to turn a blind eye to scientific knowledge. This is a sacrifice not lightly made, for the scientific attitude cannot rid itself so easily of its sense of responsibility. And if the psychologist happens to be a doctor who wants not only to classify his patient scientifically but also to understand him as a human being, he is threatened with a conflict of duties between the two diametrically opposed and mutually exclusive attitudes of knowledge, on the one hand, and understanding, on the other. This conflict cannot be solved by an either-or but only by a kind of two-way thinking: doing one thing while not losing sight of the other.

In view of the fact that in principle, the positive advantages of *knowledge* work specifically to the disadvantage of *understanding*, the judgment resulting therefrom is likely to be something of a paradox. Judged scientifically, the individual is nothing but a unit which repeats itself ad infinitum and could just as well be designated with a letter of the alphabet. For understanding, on the other hand, it is just the unique individual human being who, when stripped of all those conformities and regularities so dear to the heart of the scientist, is the supreme and only real object of investigation. The doctor, above all should be aware of this contradiction. On the one hand, he is equipped with the statistical truths of his scientific training, and on the other, he is faced with the task of treating a sick person who, especially in the case of psychic suffering, requires *individual understanding*. The more schematic the treatment is, the more resistances it—quite rightly—calls up in the patient, and the more the cure is jeopardized. The psychotherapist sees himself compelled, willy-nilly, to regard the individuality of a patient as an essential fact in the picture and to arrange his methods of treatment accordingly. Today, over the whole field of medicine, it is recognized that the task of the doctor consists in treating the sick person, not an abstract illness.

This illustration in the case of medicine is only a special instance of the problem of education and training in general. Scientific education is based in the main on statistical truths and abstract knowledge and therefore imparts an unrealistic, rational picture of the world, in which the individual, as a merely marginal phenomenon, plays no role. The individual, however, as an irrational datum, is the true and authentic carrier of reality, the *concrete* man as opposed to the unreal ideal or normal man to whom the scientific statements refer. What is more, most of the natural sciences try to represent the results of their investigations as though these had come into existence without man's intervention, in such a way that the collaboration of the psyche—an indispensable factor—remains invisible. (An exception to this is modern physics, which recognizes that the observed is not independent of the observer.) So in this respect, too, science conveys a picture of the world from which a real human psyche appears to be excluded—the very antithesis of the "humanities."

Under the influence of scientific assumptions, not only the psyche but the individual man and, indeed, all individual events whatsoever suffer a leveling down and a process of blurring that distorts the picture of reality into a conceptual average. We ought not to underestimate the psychological effect of the statistical world picture: it displaces the individual in favor of anonymous units that pile up into mass formations. Science supplies us with, instead of the concrete individual, the names of organizations and, at the highest point, the abstract idea of the State as the principle of political reality. The moral responsibility of the individual is then inevitably replaced by the policy of the State (*raison d'état*). Instead of moral and mental differentiation of the individual, you have public welfare and the raising of the living standard. The goal and meaning of individual life (which is the only *real* life) no longer lie in individual development but in the policy of the State, which is thrust upon the individual from outside and consists in the execution of an abstract idea which ultimately tends to attract all life to itself. The individual is increasingly deprived of the moral decision as to how he should live his own life, and instead is ruled, fed, clothed and educated as a social unit, accommodated in the appropriate housing unit, and amused in accordance with the standards that give pleasure and satisfaction to the masses. The rulers, in their turn, are just as much social units as the ruled and are distinguished only by the fact that they are specialized mouthpieces of the State doctrine. They do not need to be personalities capable of judgment, but thoroughgoing specialists who are unusable outside their line of business. State policy decides what shall be taught and studied. . . .

Alfred Adler (1870–1937)

The Style of Life

"The most important question of the healthy and diseased mind is not whence? but whither? Only when we know the active, directive goal of a person may we undertake to understand his movements."* Like Jung and others who came to oppose the dominant Freudian orientation in psychoanalysis, Adler took exception particularly to the method of psychogenetic reductionism which traced every action or expression to a moment in its source. In place of this biological predeterminism, Adler erected the principle of *self*-determinism—the affirmation that "the psychic life of man is determined by his goal." That principle, embodied in the concept of the "life style"—a unique pattern of purposes and projects different for every person—came to constitute the essential feature of the system of Individual Psychology which Adler founded after his break with Freud in 1910.

Adler's emphasis upon the whole character of the patient, rather than upon his symptoms, along with his recognition of the person as *consciously present* in the therapeutic encounter (as opposed to concentration upon past sources of anxiety and conflict), encouraged him to approach the patient with respect and trust; that is, to give serious consideration to his conscious explanations and reasoning.

---

*Alfred Adler, *The Practice and Theory of Individual Psychology* (New York: Harcourt, Brace, 1927), p. 244.

"Psychotherapy," he maintained, "is an exercise in cooperation and a test of cooperation. We can succeed only if we
are genuinely interested in the other. We must be able to
see with his eyes and listen with his ears."*

Although during his lifetime Adler was known primarily
for his somewhat Nietzschean doctrine of the "will to
power" and for the corollary concepts of compensation and
the "inferiority complex," it seems likely that his enduring
reputation will rest more with his insistence upon the importance of social feeling or interpersonal relations as
determinants of personal style (an emphasis carried still
further in the 1930's by the neo-Freudians generally and
by Sullivan in particular), as well as his distinctively humanistic and personalistic stress on the need to understand
the patient in therapy as a whole and unique being imbued
with purpose, with will, and with reason.

The following selection is taken from Adler's *The Science
of Living.*

IF WE LOOK AT a pine tree growing in the valley we will notice that it grows differently from one on top of a mountain.
It is the same kind of a tree, a pine, but there are two distinct
styles of life. Its style on top of the mountain is different from
its style when growing in the valley. The style of life of a
tree is the individuality of a tree expressing itself and mould-
ing itself in an environment. We recognize a style when we
see it against a background of an environment different from
what we expect, for then we realize that every tree has a life
pattern and is not merely a mechanical reaction to the environment.

It is much the same way with human beings. We see the
style of life under certain conditions of environment and it

---

*Quoted in Heinz and Rowena Ansbacher, *The Individual Psychology of
Alfred Adler* (New York: Basic Books, 1956), p. 340.

is our task to analyze its exact relation to the existing circumstances, inasmuch as mind changes with alteration of the
environment. As long as a person is in a favorable situation
we cannot see his style of life clearly. In new situations, however, where he is confronted with difficulties, the style of life
appears clearly and distinctly. A trained psychologist could
perhaps understand a style of life of a human being even
in a favorable situation, but it becomes apparent to everybody
when the human subject is put into unfavorable or difficult
situations.

Now life, being something more than a game, does not
lack difficulties. There are always situations in which human
beings find themselves confronted with difficulties. It is while
the subject is confronted with these difficulties that we must
study him and find out his different movements and characteristic distinguishing marks. As we have previously said,
the style of life is a unity because it has grown out of the
difficulties of early life and out of the striving for a goal.

But we are interested not so much in the past as in the
future. And in order to understand a person's future we must
understand his style of life. Even if we understand instincts,
stimuli, drive, etc., we cannot predict what must happen.
Some psychologists indeed try to reach conclusions by noting
certain instincts, impressions or traumas, but on closer examination it will be found that all these elements presuppose
a consistent style of life. Thus whatever stimulates, stimulates
only to *save* and *fix* a style of life.

. . . We have seen how human beings with weak organs,
because they face difficulties and feel insecure, suffer from
a feeling or complex of inferiority. But as human beings
cannot endure this for long, the inferiority feeling stimulates
them, as we have seen, to movement and action. This results
in a person having a goal. Now Individual Psychology has

long called the consistent movement toward this goal a plan of life. But because this name has sometimes led to mistakes among students, it is now called a style of life.

Because an individual has a style of life, it is possible to predict his future sometimes just on the basis of talking to him and having him answer questions. It is like looking at the fifth act of a drama, where all the mysteries are solved. We can make predictions in this way because we know the phases, the difficulties and the questions of life. Thus from experience and knowledge of a few facts we can tell what will happen to children who always separate themselves from others, who are looking for support, who are pampered and who hesitate in approaching situations. What happens in the case of a person whose goal it is to be supported by others? Hesitating, he stops or escapes the solution of the questions of life. We know how he can hesitate, stop, or escape, because we have seen the same thing happen a thousand times. We know that he does not want to proceed alone but wants to be pampered. He wants to stay far away from the great problems of life, and he occupies himself with useless things rather than struggle with the useful ones. He lacks social interests, and as a result he may develop into a problem child, a neurotic, a criminal or a suicide—that final escape. All these things are now better understood than formerly.

We realize, for instance, that in looking for the style of life of a human being we may use the normal style of life as a basis for measurement. We use the socially adjusted human being as a stand, and we can measure the variations from the normal.

At this point perhaps it would be helpful to show how we determine the normal style of life and how on the basis of it we understand mistakes and peculiarities. But before we discuss this we ought to mention that we do not count types in such studies. We do not consider human beings types because every human being has an individual style of life. Just as one cannot find two leaves of a tree absolutely identical, so one cannot find two human beings absolutely alike. Nature is so rich and the possibilities of stimuli, instincts and mistakes are so numerous, that it is not possible for two persons to be exactly identical. If we speak of types, therefore, it is only as an intellectual device to make more understandable the similarities of individuals. We can judge better if we postulate an intellectual classification like a type and study its special peculiarities. However, in doing so we do not commit ourselves to using the same classification at all times; we use the classification which is most useful for bringing out a particular similarity. People who take types and classifications seriously, once they put a person in a pigeon-hole, do not see how he can be put into any other classification.

An illustration will make our point clear. For instance when we speak of a type of individual not socially adjusted, we refer to one who leads a barren life without any social interests. This is one way of classifying individuals, and perhaps it is the most important way. But consider the individual, whose interest, however limited, is centered on visual things. Such a person differs entirely from one whose interests are largely concentrated on things oral, but both of them may be socially mal-adjusted and find it difficult to establish contact with their fellow-men. The classification by types can thus be a source of confusion if we do not realize that types are merely convenient abstractions.

Erich Fromm   (1900–   )

The Human Situation

Trained in the social sciences as well as in psychoanalysis,
Erich Fromm has transcended the conventional academic
categories and boundaries in a series of interdisciplinary
studies of man in society which might best be described
as essays in philosophical anthropology. Beginning with
Escape from Freedom (1941), Fromm has steadily elaborated his systematic perspective through such notable works
as *Man for Himself* (1947), *The Sane Society* (1955), *The
Art of Loving* (1956), *The Heart of Man* (1964), and
various other studies dealing with problems of philosophy,
religion, and contemporary politics as well as of psychology.
His writings take their departure from a philosophical
frame of reference which he has recently defined as "dialectic humanism"—an attitude marked by a "paradoxical blend
of relentless criticism, uncompromising realism, and rational faith."*

In a sense, Fromm's thought itself represents a dialectical
blend of the contrasting approaches of Marx and Freud
(along with a touch of Adler and a dollop of existentialism). His studies, especially in recent years, reveal an al-
ternation of emphasis between the "syndrome of growth"
(independence, productive love, and relatedness to others)
and the "syndrome of decay formed by love of death,

---

*Erich Fromm, *The Heart of Man: Its Genius for Good and Evil* (New York:
Harper and Row, 1964), p. 15.

incestuous symbiosis, and malignant narcissism." In *The Art of Loving*, particularly, Fromm elaborated his affirmative concept of human love as an active process consisting of "care, responsibility, respect, and knowledge"; his stress was upon the possibilities of achieving psychological freedom or autonomy through productive orientations toward the world of other selves. In *The Heart of Man*, he turned from these affirmative considerations to an examination of man's propensity for evil—that is, for destruction, hatred, and collective barbarism. His conclusion was that mankind faces an existential choice between two, and only two, possibilities: that of understanding and tolerance, of peace and community, on the one hand; and that of continued war and collective extinction on the other. The title of one of Fromm's books, *May Man Prevail?* (1961), indicates the critical contingency with which the present age is thought to be confronted: specifically, whether men in sufficient numbers possess the capacity to love and the will to choose. "Indeed," he wrote in 1964,

we must become aware in order to choose the good—but no awareness will help us if we have lost the capacity to be moved by the distress of another human being, by the friendly gaze of another person, by the song of a bird, by the greenness of grass. If man becomes indifferent to life there is no longer any hope that he can choose the good. Then, indeed, his heart will have so hardened that his "life" will be ended. If this should happen to the entire human race or to its most powerful members, then the life of mankind may be extinguished at the very moment of its greatest promise.*

The selection which follows is taken from *The Sane Society*.

M AN, IN RESPECT TO his body and his physiological functions, belongs to the animal kingdom. The functioning of the animal is determined by instincts, by specific action patterns

---

**Ibid.*, p. 150.

which are in turn determined by inherited neurological structures. The higher an animal is in the scale of development, the more flexibility of action pattern and the less completeness of structural adjustment do we find at birth. In the higher primates we even find considerable intelligence; that is, use of thought for the accomplishment of desired goals, thus enabling the animal to go far beyond the instinctively prescribed action pattern. But great as the development within the animal kingdom is, certain basic elements of existence remain the same.

The animal "is lived" through biological laws of nature; it is part of nature and never transcends it. It has no conscience of a moral nature, and no awareness of itself and of its existence; it has no reason, if by reason we mean the ability to penetrate the surface grasped by the senses and to understand the essence behind that surface; therefore the animal has no concept of the truth, even though it may have an idea of what is useful.

Animal existence is one of harmony between the animal and nature; not, of course, in the sense that the natural conditions do not often threaten the animal and force it to a bitter fight for survival, but in the sense that the animal is equipped by nature to cope with the very conditions it is to meet, just as the seed of a plant is equipped by nature to make use of the conditions of soil, climate, etcetera, to which it has become adapted in the evolutionary process.

At a certain point of animal evolution, there occurred a unique break, comparable to the first emergence of matter, to the first emergence of life, and to the first emergence of animal existence. This new event happens when in the evolutionary process, action ceases to be essentially determined by instinct; when the adaptation of nature loses its coercive character; when action is no longer fixed by hereditarily given mechanisms. When the animal transcends nature, when it transcends the purely passive role of the creature, when it becomes, biologically speaking, the most helpless animal, *man is born*. At this point, the animal has emancipated itself from nature by erect posture, the brain has grown far beyond what it was in the highest animal. This birth of man may have lasted for hundreds of thousands of years, but what matters is that a new species arose, transcending nature, that *life became aware of itself*.

Self-awareness, reason and imagination disrupt the "harmony" which characterizes animal existence. Their emergence has made man into an anomaly, into the freak of the universe. He is part of nature, subject to her physical laws and unable to change them, yet he transcends the rest of nature. He is set apart while being a part; he is homeless, yet chained to the home he shares with all creatures. Cast into this world at an accidental place and time, he is forced out of it, again accidentally. Being aware of himself, he realizes his powerlessness and the limitations of his existence. He visualizes his own end: death. Never is he free from the dichotomy of his existence: he cannot rid himself of his mind, even if he should want to; he cannot rid himself of his body as long as he is alive—and his body makes him want to be alive.

Reason, man's blessing, is also his curse; it forces him to cope everlastingly with the task of solving an insoluble dichotomy. Human existence is different in this respect from that of all other organisms; it is in a state of constant and unavoidable disequilibrium. Man's life cannot "be lived" by repeating the pattern of his species; *he* must live. Man is the only animal that can be *bored*, that can feel evicted from paradise. Man is the only animal who finds his own existence a problem which he has to solve and from which he cannot escape. He cannot go back to the prehuman state of harmony with nature; he must proceed to develop his reason until he becomes the master of nature, and of himself.

But man's birth ontogenetically as well as phylogenetically is essentially a *negative* event. He lacks the instinctive adaptation to nature, he lacks physical strength, he is the most helpless of all animals at birth, and in need of protection for a much longer period of time than any of them. While he has lost the unity with nature, he has not been given the means to lead a new existence outside of nature. His reason is most rudimentary, he has no knowledge of nature's processes, nor tools to replace the lost instincts; he lives divided into small groups, with no knowledge of himself or of others; indeed, the biblical Paradise myth expresses the situation with perfect clarity. Man, who lives in the Garden of Eden, in complete harmony with nature but without awareness of himself, begins his history by the first act of freedom, disobedience to a command. Concomitantly, he becomes aware of himself, of his separateness, of his helplessness; he is expelled from Paradise, and two angels with fiery swords prevent his return.

Man's evolution is based on the fact that he has lost his original home, nature—and that he can never return to it, can never become an animal again. There is only one way he can take: to emerge fully from his natural home, to find a new home—one which he creates, by making the world a human one and by becoming truly human himself.

When man is born, the human race as well as the individual, he is thrown out of a situation which was definite, as definite as the instincts, into a situation which is indefinite, uncertain and open. There is certainty only about the past, and about the future as far as it is death—which actually is return to the past, the inorganic state of matter.

The problem of man's existence, then, is unique in the whole of nature; he has fallen out of nature, as it were, and is still in it; he is partly divine, partly animal; partly infinite, partly finite. *The necessity to find ever-new solutions for the contradictions in his existence, to find ever-higher forms of unity with nature, his fellowmen and himself, is the source of all psychic forces which motivate man, of all his passions, affects and anxieties.*

The animal is content if its physiological needs—its hunger, its thirst and its sexual needs—are satisfied. Inasmuch as man is *also* animal, these needs are likewise imperative and must be satisfied. *But inasmuch as man is human, the satisfaction of these instinctual needs is not sufficient to make him happy; they are not even sufficient to make him sane. The archimedic point of the specifically human dynamism lies in this uniqueness of the human situation; the understanding of man's psyche must be based on the analysis of man's needs stemming from the conditions of his existence.*

The problem, then, which the human race as well as each individual has to solve is that of being born. Physical birth, if we think of the individual, is by no means as decisive and singular an act as it appears to be. It is, indeed, an important change from intrauterine into extrauterine life; but in many respects the infant after birth is not different from the infant before birth; it cannot perceive things outside, cannot feed itself; it is completely dependent on the mother, and would perish without her help. Actually, the process of birth continues. The child begins to recognize outside objects, to react affectively, to grasp things and to coordinate his movements, to walk. But birth continues. The child learns to speak, it learns to know the use and function of things, it learns to relate itself to others, to avoid punishment and gain praise and liking. Slowly, the growing person learns to love, to develop reason, to look at the world objectively. He begins to develop his powers; to acquire a sense of identity, to overcome the seduction of his senses for the sake of an integrated life. Birth then, in the conventional meaning of the word, is only the beginning of birth in the broader sense. The whole life of the individual is nothing but the process of giving birth to himself; indeed, we should be fully born, when we die—although it is the tragic fate of most individuals to die before they are born.

From all we know about the evolution of the human race, the birth of man is to be understood in the same sense as the birth of the individual. When man had transcended a certain threshold of minimum instinctive adaptation, he ceased to be an animal; but he was as helpless and unequipped for human existence as the individual infant is at birth. The birth of man began with the first members of the species homo sapiens, and human history is nothing but the whole process of this birth. It has taken man hundreds of thousands of years to take the first steps into human life; he went through a narcissistic phase of magic omnipotent orientation, through totemism, nature worship, until he arrived at the beginnings of the formation of conscience, objectivity, brotherly love. In the last four thousand years of his history, he has developed visions of the fully born and fully awakened man, visions expressed in not too different ways by the great teachers of man in Egypt, China, India, Palestine, Greece and Mexico.

The fact that man's birth is primarily a negative act, that of being thrown out of the original oneness with nature, that he cannot return to where he came from, implies that the process of birth is by no means an easy one. Each step into his new human existence is frightening. It always means to give up a secure state, which was relatively known, for one which is new, which one has not yet mastered. Undoubtedly, if the infant could think at the moment of the severance of the umbilical cord, he would experience the fear of dying. A loving fate protects us from this first panic. But at any new step, at any new stage of our birth, we are afraid again. We are never free from two conflicting tendencies: one to emerge from the womb, from the animal form of existence into a more human existence, from bondage to freedom; another, to return to the womb, to nature, to certainty and security. In the history of the individual, and of the race, the progressive tendency has proven to be stronger, yet the phenomena of mental illness and the regression of the human race to positions apparently relinquished generations ago show the intense struggle which accompanies each new act of birth.

Carl R. Rogers (1902–)

Two Divergent Trends

The author of the widely influential system known as client-centered (or nondirective) psychotherapy is a man whose professional and educational background includes liberal theology and progressive educational theory as well as a broad exposure to the major schools of psychoanalysis and clinical psychology. Carl R. Rogers moved from graduate studies at Union Theological Seminary and Columbia University Teachers College into a counseling career as director of the Rochester Guidance Center, where he remained for a dozen years before embarking upon a second career as a college professor (successively at Ohio State, Chicago, and Wisconsin). He is currently a Senior Fellow, both teaching and practicing psychotherapy, at the Western Behavioral Sciences Institute in La Jolla, California.

Despite his many years of scholarly research and theorizing, the greatest factor in shaping Rogers' approach to psychology has been his direct encounter with troubled individuals in the therapeutic relationship. Concerning this activity, he wrote in the mid-fifties: "Since 1928, for a period now approaching thirty years, I have spent probably an average of fifteen to twenty hours per week, except during vacation periods, in endeavoring to understand and be of therapeutic help to [individuals who perceive themselves, or are perceived by others to be, in need of personal help].
. . . From these hours, and from my relationships with these people I have drawn most of whatever insight I possess into

the meaning of therapy, the dynamics of interpersonal relationships, and the structure and functioning of personality."*

As a result of this intimate and sustained dialogue with
people in distress, combined with his own native endow-
ments of tolerance and trust, Rogers has developed over the
years a theory of personality and a system of psychotherapy
which depart radically from Freudian directives concerning authority and neutrality on the part of the therapist.
The three attitudes that he regards as essential to the
success of therapy are: "The realness, genuineness, or con-
gruence of the therapist; a warm, acceptant prizing of the
client, an unconditional positive regard; and a sensitive,
empathic understanding of the client's feelings that is com-
municated to the client."† Given these subjective conditions
—quite regardless of the therapist's theoretical standpoint,
the degree of his professional and scientific knowledge, or
the extent of his technical skill—Rogers believes that the
therapeutic treatment is likely to be successful and that
constructive psychological change will take place.

Rogers' affirmative and "democratic" theory of personality—for which he has expressed indebtedness to such peers
and predecessors as Rank, Goldstein, Sullivan, Maslow, May,
Allport, Snygg and Combs, and Angyal—centers upon a
conception of the person as an organized whole, striving
to actualize himself in continuous interaction with the
environment and in pursuit of goal-values. The role of
the therapist is to help the troubled client to help himself
toward further growth and freedom. It is noteworthy that in
the development of his theory and therapy, Rogers has
accumulated an impressive record of empirical and methodological substantiation, testifying to a rigorous scientific

---

*Carl R. Rogers, unpublished manuscript, quoted in *Theories of Personality*,
ed. by C. S. Hall and G. Lindzey (New York: Wiley, 1957), p. 478.

†Carl R. Rogers, 'The Therapeutic Relationship: Recent Theory and Research," *Australian Journal of Psychology*, XVII (1965), reprinted in *The
Human Dialogue: Perspectives on Communication*, ed. by F. W. Matson
and A. Montagu (New York: Free Press, 1967), p. 251.

spirit no less committed to ideals of objective validity and verifiability than the behaviorists and neo-positivists whose claim to exclusive province over the realm of mind he has persistently and persuasively challenged through nearly four decades.

THE "OBJECTIVE" TREND

On the one hand our devotion to rigorous hard-headedness in psychology, to reductionist theories, to operational definitions, to experimental procedures leads us to understand psychotherapy in purely objective rather than subjective terms. Thus we can conceptualize therapy as being simply the operant conditioning of the client. The therapist reinforces, by appropriate simple measures, those statements expressing feelings, or those which report dream content, or those which express hostility, or those which show a positive self-concept. Impressive evidence has been produced indicating that such reinforcement does increase the type of expression reinforced. Hence, the road to improvement in therapy, in this view, is to select more wisely the elements to reinforce, to have more clearly in mind the behaviors toward which we wish to shape our clients. The problem is not different in kind from Skinner's shaping of the behavior of his pigeons toward ping-pong playing.

Another variant of this general trend is what is known as the learning-theory approach to psychotherapy, which exists in several forms. Those S-R bonds are identified that are anxiety creating or that have caused difficulties in adjustment. These are labeled, and their origin and effects are interpreted and explained to the subject. Reconditioning or counterconditioning is then utilized so that the individual acquires a new, more healthy, and more socially useful response to the same stimulus that originally caused difficulty.

This whole trend has behind it the weight of current attitudes in American psychology. As I see them, these attitudes include such themes as: "Away from the philosophical and the vague. On toward the concrete, the operationally defined, the specific." "Away from anything which looks within. Our behaviors and ourselves are nothing but objects molded and shaped by conditioning circumstances. The future is determined by the past." "Since no one is free, we had better manipulate the behavior of others in an intelligent fashion, for the general good." (How unfree individuals can choose what they wish to do, and choose to manipulate others, is never made clear.) "The way to do is to *do*, quite obviously." "The way to understand is from the outside."

THE "EXISTENTIAL" TREND

Logical and natural as this trend may be, suited as it is to the temper of our culture, it is not the only trend that is evident. In Europe, which has not become so involved in scientism, and increasingly in this country, other voices are saying: "This tunnel vision of behavior is *not* adequate to the whole range of *human* phenomena." One of these voices is Abraham Maslow. Another is Rollo May. Another is Gordon Allport. There are an increasing number of others. I would like, if I may, to place myself in this group. These psychologists insist, in a variety of ways, that they are concerned with the whole spectrum of human behavior and that *human* behavior is, in some significant ways, something more than the behavior of our laboratory animals.

To illustrate this in the realm of psychotherapy, I should like to cite, very briefly, some of my own experience. I started from a thoroughly objective point of view. Psychotherapeutic treatment involved the diagnosis and analysis of the client's difficulties, the cautious interpretation and explanation to the client of the causes of his difficulties, and a re-educative process focused by the clinician upon the specific causal elements. Gradually I observed that I was more effective if I could create a psychological climate in which the client could undertake these functions himself—exploring, analyzing, understanding, and trying new solutions to his problems. During more recent years, I have been forced to recognize that the most important ingredient in creating this climate is that I should be *real*. I have come to realize that only when I am able to be a transparently real person, and am so perceived by my client, can he discover what is real in him. Then my empathy and acceptance can be effective. When I fall short in therapy, it is when I am unable to be what I deeply am. The essence of therapy, as I see it carried on by myself and by others, is a meeting of two *persons* in which the therapist is openly and freely himself and evidences this perhaps most fully when he can freely and acceptantly enter into the world of the other. Thus, borrowing from some ancient phrases, I am inclined to say, "The way to do is to *be*." "The way to understand is from within."

The result of this kind of a relationship has been well described by May. The client finds himself confirmed (to use Buber's term) not only in what he is, but in his potentialities. He can affirm himself, fearfully to be sure, as a separate, unique person. He can become the architect of his own future through the functioning of his consciousness. What this means is that because he is more open to his experience, he can permit himself to live symbolically in terms of all the possibilities. He can acceptantly live out, in his thoughts and feelings, the creative urges within himself, the destructive tendencies he finds within, the challenge of growth, the challenge of death. He can face, in his consciousness, what it will mean to him to *be*, and what it will mean to not be. He becomes an autonomous human person, able to be what he is and to choose his course. This is the outcome of therapy, as seen by this second trend.

TWO MODES OF SCIENCE

We may well ask how these different trends in therapy could come about—the one symbolized by Dollard, Miller, Rotter, Wolpe, Bergman, and others, the second by May, Maslow, myself, and others. I believe the divergence arises in part out of a differential conception of and use of science. To put it in oversimplified fashion, the learning theorist says, "We know much about how animals learn. Therapy is learning. Therefore effective therapy will be composed of what we know about animal learning." This is a perfectly legitimate use of science, projecting known findings into new and unknown fields.

The second group approaches the problem differently. These individuals are interested in observing the underlying order in therapeutic events. They say, "Some efforts to be therapeutic, to bring about constructive change, are effective; others are not. We find that there are certain characteristics that differentiate the two classes. We find, for example, that in the helpful relationships, it is likely that the therapist functions as a real person, interacting with his real feelings. In the less helpful relationships, we frequently find that the therapist functions as an intelligent manipulator, rather than as his real self." Here too is a perfectly legitimate concept of science, the detecting of the order which is inherent in any given series of events. I submit that this second conception is more likely to discover the uniquely human aspects of therapy. . . .

AN EXAMPLE

To illustrate more clearly the way in which research may clarify some of these issues, let me leap into one of the most controversial differences, and illuminate it from some studies out of the past. One of the elements of existential thinking most shocking to conventional American psychologists is that it speaks as if man were free and responsible, as though choice constituted the core of his existence. This has been evident in our speakers today. Feifel says, "Life is not genuinely our own until we can renounce it." Maslow points out that psychologists have been dodging the problem of responsibility and the place of courage in the personality. May speaks of "the agonizing burden of freedom" and the choice between being one's self or denying one's self. Certainly to many psychologists today these can never be issues with which the *science* of psychology can be concerned. They are simply speculations.

Yet bearing on precisely this point, I should like to bring in some research of a number of years ago. W. L. Kell, doing his graduate work under my supervision, chose to study the factors that would predict the behavior of adolescent delinquents.[1] He made careful objective ratings of the family climate, the educational experiences, the neighborhood and cultural influences, the social experiences, the health history, the hereditary background of each delinquent. These factors were rated as to their favorableness for normal development, on a continuum from elements destructive of the child's welfare and inimical to healthy development. Almost as an afterthought, a rating was also made of the degree of self-understanding, because it was felt that although this was not one of the primary conditioning factors, it might play some part in predicting future behavior. This was essentially a rating of the degree to which the individual was objective and realistic regarding himself and his situation, whether he was emotionally acceptant of the facts in himself and in his environment.

These ratings, on seventy-five delinquents, were compared with ratings of their behavior two to three years after the initial study. It was expected that the ratings on family climate and social experience with peers would be the best predictors of later behavior. To our amazement, the degree of self-understanding was much the best predictor, correlating .84 with later behavior, whereas quality of social experience correlated .55, and family climate .36. We simply were not prepared to believe these findings and laid the study on the shelf until it could be replicated. Later it was replicated on a new group of seventy-six cases, and all the essential findings were confirmed, though not quite so strikingly. Furthermore, the findings stood up even in detailed analysis. When we examined only the delinquents who came from the most unfavorable homes and who remained in those homes, it was still true that their future behavior was best predicted not by the unfavorable conditioning they were receiving in their home environment, but by the degree of realistic understanding of themselves and their environment that they possessed.

Here, it seems to me, is an empirical definition of what constitutes "freedom" in the sense in which Dr. May has used that term. As these delinquents were able to accept into consciousness all the facts regarding themselves and their situation, they were free to live out all the possibilities symbolically and to choose the most satisfying course of action. But those delinquents who were unable to accept reality into consciousness were compelled by the external circumstances of their lives to continue in a deviant course of behavior, unsatisfying in the long run. They were unfree. This study gives, I believe, some empirical meaning to Dr. May's statement that the "capacity for consciousness . . . constitutes the base of psychological freedom."

I have tried to point up the two diverging ways in which psychotherapy may be carried on. On the one hand, there is the strictly objective approach—nonhumanistic, impersonal, rationally based on knowledge of animal learning. On the other hand, there is the kind of approach suggested in the papers on this program, a humanistic, personal encounter in which the concern is with an "existing, becoming, emerging, experiencing being."

I have proposed that an empirical research method can study the effectiveness of each of these approaches. I have tried to indicate that the subtlety and subjective qualities of the second approach are not a barrier to its objective investigation. And I am sure that it has been clear that in my judgment the warm, subjective, human encounter of two persons is more effective in facilitating change than is the most precise set of techniques growing out of learning theory or operant conditioning.

NOTE

[1] C. R. Rogers, W. L. Kell, and H. McNeil, "The role of self-understanding in the prediction of behavior," *Jour. Consult. Psychol.*, 1948, 12, 174–186.

Harry Stack Sullivan   (1892–1949)

The Interpersonal Theory of Psychiatry

One of the great systematizers in the history of psycho-analysis and psychotherapy, Sullivan stands out among the misnamed "neo-Freudians" of the 1930's (they were self-consciously in opposition to Freud while remaining committed to his method and basic assumptions) by virtue of his distinctively American style and approach. Although trained in orthodox psychoanalysis, he was less influenced by Freud and the European schools than by the American psychobiologist Adolf Meyer, the philosopher and social psychologist George Herbert Mead, and the cultural anthropologist Edward Sapir. Both in concept and language, Sullivan resisted the Freudian style in favor of a peculiar construction of his own, replete with complicated neologisms and phrases of his invention. "Each word looks sweaty and uncomfortable," as Gerald Sykes has commented. "Linguistically, Sullivan is a true American, a product of the tongue-twisting mechanic's paradise that in earlier days gave birth to the Book of Mormon and Mary Baker Eddy."[*]

But under this heavy canopy of words was a system of psychological theory and therapy which rivaled that of Freud himself in its comprehensive sweep and brilliance. His central principle was that the adult personality is the product of social interaction, and accordingly that psychia-

---

[*]Gerald Sykes, *The Hidden Remnant* (New York: Harper, 1962), p. 103.

try is the study of "interpersonal relations"—a term which embraced not only actual life relationships with peer groups and significant others but imaginary or eidetic encounters with idealized images. Human experience generally was divided into two interrelated modes—the pursuit of satisfactions and the pursuit of security, the first devoted to biological appetites and needs, and the second concerned with the human need for acceptance and participation. Personality "dynamism," a key term for Sullivan, was defined as "the relatively enduring pattern of energy transformations which recurrently characterize the organism in its duration as a living organism."

Sullivan's major contribution on the side of therapy lies in his conception of the role of the psychiatrist not as a detached onlooker or "blank screen," as in classical psychoanalysis, but as a "participant-observer" in an interpersonal relationship with the patient which he termed the "psychiatric interview." Sullivan's unusually warm and respectful approach to the patient was an outgrowth of his pioneering work with schizophrenics, who had traditionally been regarded as beyond the reach of psychoanalytic methods. The corollary of this therapeutic empathy was a posture of active concern on the part of the analyst. "The therapist has an inescapable involvement," he wrote, "in all that goes on in the interview; and to the extent that he is unconscious or unwitting of his participation in the interview, to that extent he does not know what is happening."*

I THINK THAT THERE is no other field of scientific endeavor in which the worker's preconceptions are as troublesome as in psychiatry. To illustrate this I will give three definitions of psychiatry. The first and broadest definition would run something like this: Psychiatry is the preoccupation of psy-

---

*Sullivan, unpublished materials, quoted in Mary Julian White, "Sullivan and Treatment," in *The Contributions of Harry Stack Sullivan*, ed. by Patrick Mullahy (New York: Hermitage House, 1952), p. 121.

chiatrists; it is all that confounding conglomerate of ideas and impressions, of magic, mysticism, and information, of conceits and vagaries, of conceptions and misconceptions, and of empty verbalisms. That is the broadest definition of psychiatry and, so far as I know, a good many people are very far advanced students of that field.

Now there is a second definition which I was moved to make a good many years ago when I was attempting to find out what, if anything, I thought about psychiatry; and this is a polite definition for psychiatry of the pre-scientific era. This second definition sets up psychiatry as an art, namely, the art of observing and perhaps influencing the course of mental disorders.

The third definition of psychiatry, which is the one relevant here, may be approached by considering it as an expanding science concerned with the kinds of events or processes in which the psychiatrist participates while being an observant psychiatrist. The knowledge which is organized in psychiatry as a science is not derived from anything special about the data with which the psychiatrist deals. It arises not from a special kind of data but from the characteristic actions or operations in which the psychiatrist participates. The actions or operations from which psychiatric information is derived are events in interpersonal fields which include the psychiatrist. The events which contribute information for the development of psychiatry and psychiatric theory are events in which the psychiatrist participates; they are not events that he looks at from atop ivory towers. But of all the actions or operations in which the psychiatrist participates as a psychiatrist, the ones which are scientifically important are those which are accompanied by conceptual schematizations of intelligent formulations which are communicable. These, in turn, are those actions or operations which are relatively precise and explicit—with nothing significant left equivocal or ambiguous. . . .

The history of this field includes two tributaries which I am inclined to mention at this point in an attempt to set up as precisely as possible the reason for the interpersonal approach. Needless to say, behind all this phase of psychiatry are the discoveries of Sigmund Freud.

The first tributary is the psychobiology of Adolf Meyer. Both the Freudian discoveries and the formulae of Meyer center their attention emphatically on the individual person, as the central unit of study. Some of you may be well acquainted with the system of psychiatry which Adolf Meyer developed and to which he applied the term psychobiology. By this organization of thought, Meyer made, in my opinion, a very important contribution to the understanding of living. Before Meyer's contribution, the grand divisions of knowledge included—in the upper reaches beyond biology—psychology and sociology; and psychology was something which pertained to the mind but with the clear implication that the mind rested on concomitant physiological substrates. So psychology was a purely scientific discipline that studied something that rested on something else.

Psychobiology—and I will abstract the definition, or lack of definition, of the field provided by Meyer—is the study of man as the highest embodiment of mentally integrated life. In other words, it is a more-or-less conscious integration, which makes use of symbols and meanings. This embodiment of mentally integrated life includes the peculiar phenomenon of subject organization by which one is able to think of oneself as if objectively. While certain statements of psychobiology may seem somewhat uncertain, Meyer has stated specifically and succinctly that psychobiology is concerned with the individual human organism as a primary entity. He says that although he likes to speak of persons and groups, the person is the agent of contact. The individual has to do the choosing of his interpersonal material. The person is an object with subject capacity.

In the days when psychobiology was coming into being as a very important member of the hierarchy of knowledge—to my way of thinking a vast improvement on psychology—another discipline was being born called social psychology, which was the second tributary to the interpersonal approach. Under provocation of some very original thinking by Charles H. Cooley, George Herbert Mead, at the University of Chicago, developed a formula of social psychology which included the development of the self—not too far removed from what I discuss as the *self-system*—on the basis of reflected appraisals from others and the learning of roles which one undertook to live or "which live one"—to use a not very closely related statement of George Groddeck. The social psychology of Mead was much less vividly and utterly centered on the unique individual person. It showed very clearly that the unique individual person was a complex derivative of many others. It did not quite serve for the purpose of psychiatry as here defined, because there was, you might say, no source of energy presented to account for shifts in roles, the energy expended in playing roles, and so on. . . .

There is another field which is very powerfully tributary to the development of this theory, cultural anthropology, which is concerned with the study of the social heritage of man. I should like to refer, in this connection, to Malinowski; the briefest statement of his extremely helpful views appears in the *Encyclopaedia of the Social Sciences*. While I would like to say a good deal on this subject, I shall confine myself to one short quotation from Malinowski: "In every organized activity . . . human beings are bound together by their con-

nection with a definite portion of environment, by their
association with a common shelter and by the fact that they
carry out certain tasks in common. The concerted character
of their behavior is the result of social rules, that is, customs,
either sanctioned by explicit measures or working in an
apparently automatic way." Among the latter type of customs
are moral values, "by which man is driven to definite behavior by inner compulsion," to quote Malinowski again.
Without considerable help from the student of cultural anthropology on such massive questions as language, for example, I believe that it is impossible at all readily to pass
from the field of psychobiology and social psychology, as
defined, to that of psychiatry as here defined.

And finally, I believe that there is also an absolutely necessary convergence of social psychology as the study of interpersonal interaction, and of psychiatry as the study of interpersonal interaction—a tautology which I hope you will
forgive me. As a psychiatrist, I had come to feel over the
years that there was an acute need for a discipline which
was determined to study not the individual human organism
or the social heritage, but the interpersonal situations
through which persons manifest mental health or mental
disorder. Approaching it from another viewpoint, Leonard
Cottrell, who has, I think, carried social psychology a long
way, came to the conclusion that investigations in social
psychology had to be made within the frame of reference
of interpersonal situations.

In my attempt to outline such a field, I discovered that it
seemed to be the field in which the activity—the actions and
the operations—of a psychiatrist could be given communicable
conceptual schematization, and, therefore, seekable scientific
meaning.

It is, I believe, perfectly correct to say with Bridgman

". . . I act in two modes . . . my public mode . . . and in the private mode, [in which] I feel my inviolable isolation from my fellows. . . ." Psychiatry studies, as I see it, activity in the public mode and also that part of activity in the private mode which is not in any sense inviolably isolated. Let me say that insofar as you are interested in your unique individuality, in contradistinction to the interpersonal activities which you or someone else can observe, to that extent you are interested in the really private mode in which you live—in which I have no interest whatever. The fact is that for any scientific inquiry, in the sense that psychiatry should be, we cannot be concerned with that which is inviolably private. The setting up of the psychiatric field as a study of interpersonal relations is certainly necessary if psychiatry is to be scientific; furthermore, by this simple expedient of so defining psychiatry, we weed out from the serious psychiatric problems a great number of pseudo-problems—which, since they are pseudo-problems, are not susceptible of solution, attempts at their solution being, in fact, only ways of passing a lifetime pleasantly. Let me repeat that psychiatry as a science cannot be concerned with anything which is immutably private; it must be concerned only with the human living which is in, or can be converted into, the public mode.

Thus as psychobiology seeks to study the individual human being, and as cultural anthropology, which has been a powerful tributary to social science, seeks to study the social heritage shown in the concerted behavior of people making up a group, so psychiatry—and its convergent, social psychology—seeks to study the biologically and culturally conditioned, but *sui generis*, interpersonal processes occurring in the interpersonal situations in which the observant psychiatrist does his work.

Ludwig Binswanger (1881–   )

Existential Analysis and Psychotherapy

"If Nietzsche and psychoanalysis have shown that instinctuality, especially in the form of sexuality, extends its reach up to the highest pinnacles of human spirituality, then we have attempted to show the degree to which spirituality extends its reach down to the deepest valleys of 'vitality.' "* Ludwig Binswanger, born into a Swiss family distinguished for several generations of psychiatrists and physicians, is the founder of a school of existential psychoanalysis which some believe to represent a third "Copernican Revolution" rivaling and counterbalancing that of Freud. An intimate of both Freud and Jung (he took his medical degree under Jung at Zurich in 1907), Binswanger gained wide attention in 1958 for the English edition of his *Sigmund Freud: Reminiscences of a Friendship.* That friendship was remarkable principally for surviving profound theoretical differences between the two psychoanalysts—differences at least as great as those which led to traumatic breaks between Freud and such of his colleagues as Jung, Adler, Stekel, Rank, and Ferenczi. Both the differences and the affectionate bond that existed between Binswanger and Freud are illuminated by a letter of Freud's responding to an address which Binswanger delivered in 1936 in commemoration of Freud's eightieth birthday:

---

*Quoted in *Being-in-the-World: Selected Papers of Ludwig Binswanger*, translated and edited by Jacob Needleman (New York: Basic Books, 1963), p. 3.

Dear Friend! A sweet surprise, your lecture! Those who heard you and reported to me were visibly untouched by it; it must have been too difficult for them. In reading it I rejoiced over your beautiful prose, your erudition, the scope of your horizon, your tact in disagreement. Truly, one can put up with infinite amounts of praise.

But, of course, I don't believe a word of what you say. *I've always lived only in the* parterre *and basement of the building. You claim that with a change of viewpoint one is able to see an upper story which houses such distinguished guests as religion, art, etc. You're not the only one who thinks that, most cultured specimens of* homo natura *believe it. In that you are conservative, I revolutionary. If I had another lifetime of work before me, I have no doubt that I could find room for these noble guests in my little subterranean house. . . ."*

Binswanger might well have replied that, however dark and formidable the basement, it is still part of the house that man built. While not disregarding the instinctual side of human existence, he chooses to emphasize that this existence (and these instincts) are *human*. Psychology and psychotherapy, in this existentialist perspective, are concerned not just with instinctual man, or frustrated man, or mentally ill man, but with "man as such"—with the whole man, or Man in Person (as Lewis Mumford has phrased it). In company with the major existentialist thinkers in philosophy as well as in psychology, Binswanger's concern is to avoid the reduction of the human patient into an object to be dissected and categorized. "The new understanding of man," he writes, "which we owe to Heidegger's analysis of existence, has its basis in the conception that man is no longer understood in terms of some theory—be it a mechanistic, a biologic or a psychological one." The existentially oriented analyst, therefore, whatever his formal affiliation or school, "will not degrade the patient to an object toward which he is subject, but he will see in him an existential partner." This commitment to what Martin Buber called the I-Thou relation of person to person, meeting together

---

Ibid., pp. 3–4.

on "the sharp edge of existence," entails obvious risks for the therapist. Binswanger's recognition of this therapeutic contingency is expressed in his injunction to the psychotherapist that he "must dare to risk committing his own existence in the struggle for the freedom of his partner's."

ZURICH IS THE BIRTHPLACE of existential analysis (*Daseins-analyse*) as a psychiatric-phenomenologic research method. I emphasize the term *research method,* for if the psychoanalytic theory of Freud or the teaching of Jung arose out of a dissatisfaction with preceding psychotherapy, thus owing their origin and development predominantly to psychotherapeutic impulses and aims, the existential research orientation in psychiatry arose from dissatisfaction with the prevailing efforts to gain scientific understanding in psychiatry; so that existential analysis owes its origin and development to an attempt to gain a new scientific understanding of the concerns of psychiatry, psychopathology and psychotherapy, on the basis of the analysis of existence (*Daseinsanalytik*) as it was developed in the remarkable work of Martin Heidegger: "Being and Time" (*Sein und Zeit*), in the year 1927. Psychology and psychotherapy, as sciences, are admittedly concerned with "man," but not at all primarily with mentally *ill* man, but with *man as such.* The new understanding of man, which we owe to Heidegger's analysis of existence, has its basis in the new conception that man is no longer understood in terms of some theory—be it a mechanistic, a biologic or a psychological one—but in terms of a purely phenomenologic elucidation of the total structure or total articulation of existence as BEING-IN-THE-WORLD (*In-der-Welt-sein*). What this expression, fundamental for existential analysis, means, I unfortunately cannot develop here; be it only

emphasized that it encompasses alike the individual's own
world and the simultaneous and coextensive relationships
with and to other people and things. Nor can I go into the
difference between an ontologic-phenomenologic analysis of
existence, an empiric-phenomenologic existential analysis, and
an empiric discursive description, classification and explanation.

Once, in his interpretation of dreams, Freud said that
psychiatrists had "forsaken the stability of the psychic structure too early." Existential analysis could say the same thing,
albeit with an altogether different meaning. Freud, as is well
known, had in mind the stability of the articulation of the
life-history with the psychic structure, in contrast to the
psychiatrists of his day who, at the very first opportunity,
considered the psychic structure to be disrupted, and who
resorted instead to physiologic processes in the cerebral cortex. Existential analysis, on the other hand, does not have in
mind the solidity of the structure of the inner life-history, but
rather the solidity of the transcendental structure preceding
or underlying, a priori, all psychic structures as the very
condition of this possibility. I regret that I cannot explain
in fuller detail these philosophic expressions, already employed by Kant but here used in a much wider sense; those
among you conversant with philosophy will readily understand me. I want to emphasize only that philosophy is not
here in any way being introduced into psychiatry or psychotherapy, but rather that the philosophic bases of these sciences
are being laid bare. Obviously, this in turn has an effect upon
one's understanding of what constitutes their scientific object
or field. This effect reveals itself in the fact that we have
learned to understand and to describe the various psychoses
and neuroses as specific *deviations* of the a priori, or the

transcendental, structure of man's humanity, of the *condition humaine*, as the French say.

Be it noted in passing that the existential-analytic research method in psychiatry had to investigate the structure of existence as being-in-the-world, as Heidegger had outlined and delineated it still further and along various new paths. Such, for instance, are its studies of various existential "dimensions," i.e., height, depth and width, thingness and resistance (*Materialität*), lighting and coloring of the world, fullness or emptiness of existence, etc. The investigation of psychotic or neurotic world-projects and existential structures such as, for example, those which we designate as manic, depressive, schizophrenic, or compulsive, have so occupied all of us who are engaged upon this work that only suggestions are at hand with regard to the significance of existential-analytic research for psychotherapy. I should like now very cursorily to indicate a few of the main trends of this relationship.

(1) A psychotherapy on existential-analytic bases investigates the life-history of the patient to be treated, just as any other psychotherapeutic method, albeit in its own fashion. It does not explain this life-history and its pathologic idiosyncrasies according to the teachings of any school of psychotherapy, or by means of its preferred categories. Instead, it *understands* this life-history as modifications of the total structure of the patient's being-in-the-world, as I have shown in my studies "On Flight of Ideas" (*Über Ideenflucht*), in my studies of schizophrenia, and most recently in the case of "Suzanne Urban."

(2) A psychotherapy on existential-analytic bases thus proceeds *not* merely by showing the patient where, when and to what extent he has failed to realize the fullness of his humanity, but it tries to make him *experience* this as radically

as possible—how, like Ibsen's master-builder, Solness, he has lost his way and footing in "airy heights" or "ethereal worlds of fantasy." In this case the psychotherapist could be compared to someone who is informed, e.g., a mountain guide, familiar with the particular terrain, who attempts the trip back to the valley with the unpracticed tourist who no longer dares either to proceed or to return. And inversely, the existential-analytically-oriented therapist seeks to enable the depressed patient to get out of his cavernous subterranean world, and to gain footing "upon the ground" once more, by revealing it to him as being the only mode of existence in which the fullness of human possibilities can be realized. And further, the existential-analytically-oriented therapist will lead the twisted schizophrenic out of the autistic world of distortion and askewness in which he lives and acts, into the shared worlds, the *koinos kosmos* of Heraclitus; or he will strive to help a patient who, in her own words, lives "in two speeds" to "synchronize" these (again using her own expression). Yet, another time the therapist will see (as happened in one of Roland Kuhn's cases of anorexia mentalis) that the goal may be reached much more rapidly if one explores not the temporal but the spatial structures of a particular patient's world. It came as a surprise to us to find how easily some otherwise not particularly intelligent or educated patients proved accessible to an existential-analytic kind of exploration, and how thoroughly they felt understood by it in their singularity. This is, after all, an altogether indispensable prerequisite for any kind of psychotherapeutic success.

(3) Regardless of whether the existential analyst is predominantly psychoanalytic or predominantly jungian in orientation, he will always stand on the same plane with his patients—the plane of common existence. He will therefore

not degrade the patient to an object toward which he is subject, but he will see in him an existential partner. He will therefore not consider the bond between the two partners to be as that of two electric batteries—a "pyschic contact"—but as an *encounter* on what Martin Buber calls the "sharp edge of existence," an existence which *essentially* "is in the world," not merely as a self but also as a being-together with one another—relatedness and love. Also what has, since *Freud*, been called transference is, in the existential-analytic sense, a kind of encounter. For encounter is a being-with-others in *genuine presence*, that is to say, in the present which is altogether continuous with the *past* and bears within it the possibilities of a *future*.

(4) Perhaps you will also be interested in hearing what is the position of existential analysis toward the *dream*, and this again particularly with regard to psychotherapy. Here again it is removed from any theoretic "explanation" of the dream, especially from the purely sexual exegesis of dream contents in psychoanalysis; rather, it understands the dream, as I emphasized a long time ago, as a specific way of being-in-the-world, in other words, as a specific world and a specific way of existing. This amounts to saying that in the dream we see the whole man, the *entirety* of his problems, in a different existential modality than in waking, but against the background and with the structure of the a priori articulation of existence, and therefore the dream is also of paramount therapeutic importance for the existential analyst. For precisely by means of the structure of dreams he is enabled first of all to show the patient the structure of his being-in-the-world in an over-all manner, and secondly, he can, on the basis of this, free him for the *totality* of existential possibilities of being, in other words, for open resoluteness (*Entschlossenheit*); he can, to use Heidegger's expression, "retrieve"

(*zurückholen*) existence from a dream existence to a genuine capacity for being itself. For the time being, I will refer you to Roland Kuhn's paper, "On the Existential Structure of a Neurosis" in Gebsattel's *Jahrbuch für Psychologie und Psychotherapie*. I only ask of you not to imagine existential structure as something static, but as something undergoing constant change. Similarly, what we call neurosis represents a changed existential *process*, as compared with the healthy. Thus, existential analysis understands the task of psychotherapy to be the opening up of new structural possibilities to such altered existential processes.

As you see, existential analysis, instead of speaking in theoretic concepts, such as "pleasure principle" and "reality principle," investigates and treats the mentally-ill person with regard to the structures, structural articulations and structural alterations of his existence. Hence, it has not, by any means, consciousness as its sole object, as has been erroneously stated, but rather the whole man, prior to any distinction between conscious and unconscious, or even between body and soul; for the existential structures and their alterations permeate man's entire being. Obviously, the existential analyst, insofar as he is a therapist, will not, at least in the beginning of his treatment, be able to dispense with the distinction between conscious and unconscious, deriving from the psychology of consciousness and bound up with its merits and its drawbacks.

(5) Taking stock of the relationship between existential analysis and psychotherapy, it can be said that existential analysis cannot, over long stretches, dispense with the traditional psychotherapeutic methods; that, however, it can, as such, be therapeutically effective only insofar as it succeeds in opening up to the sick fellow man an understanding of the structure of human existence, and allows him to find his

way back from his neurotic or psychotic, lost, erring, perforated or twisted mode of existence and world, into the freedom of being able to utilize his own capacities for existence. This presupposes that the existential analyst, insofar as he is a psychotherapist, not only is in possession of existential-analytic and psychotherapeutic competence, but that he must dare to risk committing his own existence in the struggle for the freedom of his partner's.

PART V ooo

The Spire:

Philosophy as Psychology

Friedrich Nietzsche (1844–1900)

The Will to Power

Sigmund Freud is reported by his biographer Ernest Jones to have remarked on various occasions that it was Nietzsche who "had a more penetrating knowledge of himself than any other man who ever lived or was ever likely to live." However that may be, there is little doubt that Nietzsche was at once a great psychologist and a great subject for psychologizing—the former in works like *Beyond Good and Evil* and *Ecce Homo* (wherein he analyzed himself), the latter in works like *Thus Spake Zarathustra*, of which it has been remarked that "perhaps no other book contains such a steady procession of images, symbols, and visions straight out of the unconscious."* Always a lonely, troubled and physically racked individual, Nietzsche finally succumbed to psychosis at the age of forty-five; but his tragic denouement should not obscure the profoundly affirmative and exuberant side of his nature, the "Dionysian" mood which characterized the largest part of his writing. His aversion to hypocrisy and cant, his sweeping condemnation of the philistines of religion and philosophy whose self-righteous moralizing masked an underlying immorality, and above all his fierce independence of thought and action, exerted an influence upon such diverse figures as Shaw, Gide, Mann, Heidegger, and Sartre, along with psychologists like Freud and Otto Rank. It is well known that he

---

*William Barrett, *Irrational Man* (Garden City: Doubleday Anchor Books, 1958), p. 167.

also came to be embraced by the Nazis in the Hitler period, although this gesture represented an obviously opportune (not to say cynical) misperception of Nietzsche's philosophical doctrine of the Will to Power.

In his conception of the will to power as the essential motivation of man, Nietzsche anticipated the psychologies of Adler and Rank with their emphasis upon the power drive and upon the capacity of the individual will to determine the direction of life. He was also making a chilling diagnosis of modern civilization with its celebration of acquisitive urges and competitive egoism—its vast technological achievements side by side with the loss of community and the advent of alienation, anomie, and nihilism. "What I relate is the history of the next two centuries," he wrote in the preface to *The Will to Power*. "I describe what is coming, what can no longer come differently: *the advent of nihilism*. . . . Our whole European culture is moving for some time now, with a tortured tension that is growing from decade to decade, as toward a catastrophe: restlessly, violently, headlong, like a river that wants to reach the end, that no longer reflects, that is afraid to reflect."

Beyond Good and Evil, from which our selection has been taken, might be described as a psychology of ethics, a companion-piece to his other book *The Genealogy of Morals*. Full of mockery, even of trickery, Nietzsche's apparently rambling and aphoristic style disguises a systematic method of analysis and criticism which lays bare the posturings and rationalizations of the Experts and opens the way to a fresh inquiry into the authentic ground of truly human values. "Why has the advent of nihilism become necessary?" he asked. "Because the values we have had hitherto thus draw their final consequence; because nihilism represents the ultimate logical conclusion of our great values and ideals—because we must experience nihilism before we can find out what value these 'values' really had.—We require, at some time, new values."*

The Will to Power, quoted in Walter Kaufmann (ed.), *Existentialism from Dostoevsky to Sartre* (New York: Meridian Books, 1956), p. 110.

Wandering through the many fine and coarse moralities which have hitherto ruled on earth, as well as those which still rule, I found certain features regularly occurring together and bound up with one another. Finally they revealed two basic types to me, and a basic difference leaped to my eye. There is *master-morality* and *slave-morality*: I add immediately that in all higher and mixed cultures there are also attempts at a mediation between these two, and even more frequently a mix-up of them and a mutual misunderstanding; at times in fact a relentless juxtaposition even within the psyche of a single individual. The moral value-differentiations arose either among a ruling type which was pleasantly conscious of its difference from the ruled—or else among the ruled, the slaves and dependents of all kinds. In the first case, when the rulers determine the concept "good," it is the elevated and proud conditions of the psyche which are felt to be what excels and determines the order of rank. The distinguished human being divorces himself from the being in whom the opposite of such elevated and proud conditions is expressed. He despises them. One may note immediately that in the first type of morality the antithesis "good vs. bad" means "distinguished vs. despicable"; the antithesis "good vs. evil" has a different origin. What is despised is the coward, the timid man, and the petty man, he who thinks in terms of narrow utility; likewise the suspicious man with his cowed look, the one who humiliates himself, the dog-type who lets himself be mistreated, the begging flatterer, and above all the liar: it is the basic faith of all aristocrats that the common people are liars. "We truthful ones" the nobles called themselves in ancient Greece. It is obvious that the moral value-characteristics are at first applied to *people* and only later, in a transferred sense, to *acts*. This is why it is

a sad mistake when moral historians begin with questions
like "Why was the compassionate act praised?" The distinguished type of human being feels *himself* as value-
determining; he does not need to be ratified; he judges that
"which is harmful to me is harmful as such"; he knows that
he is the something which gives honor to objects; he *creates
values*. This type honors everything he knows about himself;
his morality is self-glorification. In the foreground is the feeling of fullness, of power that would flow forth, the bliss of
high tension, the consciousness of riches which would like to
give and lavish. The distinguished man, too, helps the unhappy, but not—at least not mainly—from compassion, but
more from an internal pressure that has been built up by
an excess of power. The distinguished man honors himself in
the mighty, including those who have power over themselves;
those who know when to talk and when to keep silent; those
who take delight in being rigorous and hard with themselves
and who have respect for anything rigorous and hard.
"Wotan placed a hard heart in my breast," says an old
Scandinavian saga: this is the proper poetic expression for
the soul of a proud Viking. Such a type of man is proud *not*
to have been made for compassion; hence the hero of the
saga adds a warning: "Whoever has not a hard heart when
young will never get it at all." Distinguished and courageous
men with such thoughts are at the opposite end from that
morality which sees the characteristic function of morality in
pity or in doing for others or *désintéressement*. Belief in oneself, pride in oneself, basic hostility and irony against "self-
lessness" is as sure a part of distinguished morality as an easy
disdain and cautious attitude toward the fellow-feelings and
the "warm heart." It is the powerful men who *understand*
how to accord honor: that is their art, the domain of their
invention. Profound respect for old age and for origins: their

whole law stands on this twofold respect. Faith in and pre-possession for one's ancestors and prejudice against the future ones is typical of the morality of the powerful. Contrariwise, when men of "modern ideas" believe almost instinctively in "progress" and in "the future" and have less and less respect for the old, that alone reveals clearly enough the undistinguished origin of their "ideas." But the point at which the morality of rulers is most foreign to current taste and most painstakingly strict in principle is this: one has duties only toward one's equals; toward beings of a lower rank, toward everything foreign to one, one may act as one sees fit, "as one's heart dictates"—in any event, "beyond good and evil." The ability and the duty to sustain enduring gratitude and enduring vengefulness—both only toward one's equals; subtlety in requital and retaliation; a subtly refined concept of friendship; a certain need to have enemies (as outlets for the passions: envy, quarrelsomeness and wantonness—basically, in order to be capable of being a good *friend*): all these are typical marks of the distinguished type of morality which, as I have indicated, is not the morality of "modern ideas" and hence is difficult today to empathize with, and equally difficult to dig out and uncover. The situation is different with the second type of morality, the slave morality. Assuming that the violated ones, the oppressed, the suffering, the unfree, those who are uncertain and tired of themselves—assuming that they moralize: What will they have in common in their moral evaluations? Probably a pessimistic suspiciousness against the whole situation of mankind will appear; perhaps a judgment against mankind together with its position. The eye of the slave looks unfavorably upon the virtues of the powerful; he *subtly* mistrusts all the "good" that the others honor—he would like to persuade himself that even their happiness is not real. Conversely, those qualities are emphasized and illuminated which serve to make existence easier for the sufferers: here compassion, the complaisant helping hand, the warm heart, patience, diligence, humility and friendliness are honored, for these are the useful qualities and almost the only means for enduring the pressure of existence. Slave-morality is essentially a utility-morality. Here is the cornerstone for the origin of that famous antithesis "good vs. evil." Power and dangerousness, a certain frightfulness, subtlety and strength which do not permit of despisal, are felt to belong to evil. Hence according to slave morality, the "evil" man inspires fear; according to master morality, the "good" man does and wants to, whereas the "bad" man is felt to be despicable. The antithesis reaches its sharpest point when ultimately the "good" man within a slave morality becomes the logical target of a breath of disdain—however slight and well-meaning, because he is the *undangerous* element in his morality: good natured, easily deceived, perhaps a little stupid, *un bonhomme*. Whenever slave morality preponderates, language shows a tendency to reconcile the meanings of "good" and "dumb." A final basic distinction is that the longing for *freedom*, the instinct for happiness and the subtleties of the freedom-feelings belong as necessarily to slave morality as skill and enthusiasm for reverence, for devotion, is the regular symptom of an aristocratic manner of thinking and evaluating. This enables us to understand easily why love *as passion* (our European specialty) must be of distinguished origin; we know it was invented by the Provençal knightly poets, those magnificent inventive men of *gai saber*—to whom Europe owes so much, and almost itself. . . .

.   .   .

The more a psychologist—a born, irrepressible psychologist and soul-diviner—turns his attention to the more select cases and human beings, the greater becomes the danger that he will choke on compassion. He *needs* hardness and gay serenity more than other men. For the perishableness, the destructability, of superior human beings, of the rarer psychic types, is the rule: it is horrifying to have such a rule always before one's eyes. The psychologist who, at first once and then almost always and throughout history, discovers this destructability, the whole inner incurability of the superior man, his everlasting "too late" in every sense, suffers a complex martyrdom which some day may cause him to turn against his own fate and attempt to destroy himself—to "perish." In almost every psychologist one will find a revealing inclination toward and pleasure in dealing with everyday, well-ordered human beings. What he reveals with this is that he always needs healing himself, that he needs a kind of escape and forgetting, away from the burdens that his insights and incisions, his "trade," have placed on his conscience. He is characterized by a fear of his own memory. He easily becomes silent when he hears the judgment of others; with an unmoved face he listens to them honoring, admiring loving, and transfiguring something that he has *seen*—or else he hides even his silence by expressly agreeing with some foreground-opinion. Perhaps the paradox of his position goes so far toward the gruesome, that the masses, the educated people, the enthusiasts, learn their great reverence just where he has learned his great compassion plus his great contempt— the reverence for "great men," for the rare creatures for whose sake one blesses and honors one's fatherland, the earth, all human dignity, oneself; toward whom one guides and educates the youth. . . . And who knows whether the same thing did not happen in all the great cases thus far: the masses adored a god, and the "god" was only a poor sacrificial animal. Success has always been the worst of liars and even "works" are a form of success; the great statesman, the con-

queror, the discoverer are all disguised by their own creations to the point of unrecognizability; the "work" of the
artist, the philosopher, really invents him who created it—
who is supposed to have created it; the "great men" as they
are honored are small poor fictions after the fact; in the
world of historical values it is counterfeiting that rules.
These great poets, for example, these Byrons, Mussets, Poes,
Leopardis, Kleists, Gogols (I don't dare mention the greater
names but I mean them) —such as they are and perhaps have
to be, are men of the moment, enthusiastic, sensual, child-
brained, equally irresponsible and precipitous in suspiciousness and confidence, the owners of souls that usually contain
some kind of a fissure, often avenging in their works an inner
defilement, often seeking release from an all too faithful
memory, often lost in the swamps and almost in love with
the swamps until they become like will-o'-the-wisps and can
pretend to be stars—the people then call them idealists—often
struggling with a longlasting nausea, with an oft-returning
ghost of unbelief that makes them cold and forces them to
pant after "glory" and to eat "faith in themselves (and a
such)" out of the hands of ecstatic flatterers—what a torture
are these great artists and superior men in general for one
who has found them out! It is so easy to understand how
they receive those outbreaks of boundless and utterly devoted
compassion from women—women being clairvoyant in the
world of suffering and unfortunately possessed of a mania for
helping and saving that which is far beyond their actual
power to help and save. The masses, particularly the masses
who honor and respect the artist, do not understand this
phenomenon and overwhelm it with inquisitive and self-
complaisant interpretations. The compassion of women is
regularly deceived in its powers; they would like to believe
that love can do anything—it is their characteristic *superstition*. Alas, whoever knows the human heart guesses how

poor, helpless, pretentious, and blundering even the best and deepest love is—it destroys more easily than it saves! It is possible that beneath the holy fable and disguise of the life of Jesus there is hidden one of the most painful instances of the martyrdom of the most innocent and greedy heart that never ever got enough of human love, the heart that *demanded* nothing other than love, than being loved; who turned hardness, insanity, and frightful explosions against all who denied their love; the history of a poor unsated and insatiable creature of love who had to invent hell in order to send those who didn't *want* to love him there—who finally, after he had become knowing in human love, had to invent a God who is entirely love, entirely *able* to love, who takes pity on human love because it is so wretched, so unknowing! Whoever feels this way, whoever *knows* love in this fashion—*seeks* death. But why ponder such painful matters? Assuming that one does not have to. . . .

Karl Jaspers (1883–   )

Man in the Modern Age: Existence-Philosophy

The stature of Karl Jaspers among modern-day existentialist thinkers is suggested by the statement of one reputable historian that "First place among the philosophers of existence is due to Karl Jaspers, the originator of the movement."[*] However disputable this claim may be, it is clear that the founder of *Existenzphilosophie* is at the center of the twentieth-century movement of psychological philosophy which stands deliberately in opposition to the various forms of scientific positivism bequeathed to philosophy and the social studies by the century of Comte and Darwin. Moreover, his professional career and training give him a peculiar relevance to an anthology concerned with the study of mind and the reach of psychology; before turning to philosophy he had taken a medical degree, was an assistant at the Psychiatric Clinic in Heidelberg, and assumed his first teaching position as a lecturer in psychology. His first important publication was a *General Psychopathology* (1913) and his second work, still more influential, was the *Psychology of World-Views* (1919). It may have been this psychological awareness and experience which guided Jaspers in his later philosophic phase into an attitude of profound concern for the freedom and

---

[*]F. H. Heinemann, *Existentialism and the Modern Predicament* (New York: Harper Torchbooks, 1958), p. 59.

authentic existence of the individual human person. Whether he is examining the traditional doctrines of the great philosophers, or appraising the problematic condition of man in the modern age, the point of departure for Jaspers is always his firm conception of the courageous, independent, and self-chosen person.

In *Man in the Modern Age*, published in 1931, Jaspers devoted his attention to what he regarded as the overriding problem of contemporary civilization—the crisis of individuality in the mass society. Like Kierkegaard and Nietzsche before him, like all the existentialist philosophers of his own time—and most of all like Gabriel Marcel (*Man Against Mass Society*) and Nicholas Berdyaev (*The Fate of Man in the Modern World*)—Jaspers exposed the progressive alienation and ultimate extinction of the person as a responsible and self-determining agent beneath the onslaught of mechanization and bureaucracy. "Thus the basic problem of our time," he concluded, "is whether an independent human being in his self-comprehended destiny is still possible. Indeed, it has become a general problem whether man can be free. . . ." But the possibility of freedom, of authentic selfhood, remains open; and we can never quite accept the prophecies of doom which would close the door against that opportunity.

The contemplation of a world of complete unfaith, a world in which men have been degraded to the level of machines and have lost thir own selves and their Godhead, a world in which human nobility will have been scattered and dispersed and in the end utterly ruined, is possible to us only in the formal sense, and for a fleeting moment. Just as it conflicts with the inward unfathomable dignity of man to think that he must die, must become as if he had never been, so likewise does he find it impossible to accept for more than a moment the conviction that his freedom, his faith, his self-hood will cease to be, and that he will be degraded to become a mere cog-wheel in a technical apparatus. Man is something more than he can vision in such perspectives.*

---

*Karl Jaspers, *Man in the Modern Age* (Garden City: Doubleday Anchor, 1957), pp. 227–228.

Sociology, psychology, and anthropology teach that man is to be regarded as an object concerning which something can be learnt that will make it possible to modify this object by deliberate organisation. In this way one comes to know something about man, without coming to know man himself; yet man, as a possibility of a creature endowed with spontaneity, rises in revolt against being regarded as a mere result. What the individual can be transformed into sociologically or psychologically or anthropologically, is not accepted by him as cogent without qualification. By comprehending cognisable reality as something particular and relative, he emancipates himself from that which the sciences would like definitively to make of him. He perceives that the transgression of the limits of the cognisable by way of a dogmatic self-assertion of known being is nothing more than a deceptive substitute for true philosophy, and that those who wish to escape from freedom seek justification for their action in a spurious knowledge of being.

For his activities in every situation and in all occupations, man needs a specific expert knowledge concerning things and concerning himself as life. But expert knowledge alone is never adequate for it only becomes significant in virtue of him who possesses it. The use I make of it is primarily determined by my own will. The best laws, the most admirable institutions, the most trustworthy acquirements of knowledge, the most effective technique, can be used in conflicting ways. They are of no avail unless individual human beings fulfil them with an effective and valuable reality. What actually happens, therefore, cannot be modified merely by an improvement in expert knowledge; only through man's being can it be decisively altered. Decisive is a man's inward attitude, the way in which he contemplates his world and

grows aware of it, the essential value of his satisfactions—
these things are the origin of what he does.

Existence-philosophy is the way of thought by means of
which man seeks to become himself; it makes use of expert
knowledge while at the same time going beyond it. This way
of thought does not cognise objects, but elucidates and makes
actual the being of the thinker. Brought into a state of sus-
pense by having transcended the cognitions of the world (as
the adoption of a philosophical attitude towards the world)
that fixate being, it appeals to its own freedom (as the elucidation of existence) and gains space for its own unconditioned activity through conjuring up Transcendence (as
metaphysics).

This existence-philosophy cannot be rounded off in any
particular work, nor can it acquire definitive perfectionment
as the life of any particular thinker. It was, in modern times,
originated by Kierkegaard, and through him procured widespread diffusion. During his lifetime he had created a sensation in Copenhagen, but thereafter had passed into oblivion.
Shortly before the Great War, people began to talk about
him once more, but his period of effective influence has only
just begun. Schelling, in the later development of his philosophical thought, entered paths on which, existentially, he
made a breach in German idealism. But whilst Kierkegaard
sought vainly for a method of communication, and made use
for this purpose of the technique of the pseudonym and of
his method of "psychological experiment," Schelling on the
other hand buried his sound impulses and views in the
idealistic systematisation which, having developed it in his
youth, he was unable to rid himself of. Whereas Kierkegaard
deliberately concerned himself with the most fundamental
problem of philosophy, that of communication, and while
aiming at achieving a means of indirect communication ac-

tually arrived at a strangely defective result (which nevertheless cannot fail to stimulate the reader), Schelling hardly became aware of what he was driving at, and his meaning is only discoverable by those who have acquired Kierkegaard's light. Nietzsche's road towards existence-philosophy took its rise independently of these two earlier thinkers. Anglo-Saxon pragmatism was a sort of preliminary stage. In its assault against traditional idealism, Pragmatism seemed to be laying new foundations; but what it built thereon was nothing more than an aggregate of crude analysis of life and cheap optimism, was a mere expression of a blind confidence in the extant confusion.

Existence-philosophy cannot discover any solution, but can only become real in the multiplicity of thought proceeding from extant origins in the communication from one to another. It is timely, but is already more obvious in its failures than in its successes, and has already succumbed to the premature tumultuousness with which everything significant that enters the contemporary world is greeted.

Existence-philosophy would be instantly lost if it were once more to imply a belief that we know what man is. It would again provide outlines for the study of the types of human and animal life, would again become anthropology, psychology, sociology. It can only have a possible significance so long as the objects at which it is to direct its attention are not laid down and limited exclusively. It awakens what it does not itself know; it elucidates and gives impetus, but it does not fixate. For the man who is on the right road it is the expression thanks to which he is enabled to maintain his direction; it is the instrument whereby he is empowered to safeguard his sublime moments of realisation throughout life.

Existence-philosophy may lapse into pure subjectivity. Then selfhood is misunderstood as the being of the ego, which solipsistically circumscribes itself as life that wishes to be nothing more. But genuine existence-philosophy is that appealing questioning in which, to-day, man is again seeking to come to his true self. Obviously, therefore, it is found only where people wrestle on its behalf. Out of a chance-medley with sociological, psychological, and anthropological thought, it may degenerate into a sophistical masquerade. Now censured as individualism, now used as a justification for personal shamelessness, it becomes the perilous foundation of a hysterical philosophy. But where it remains genuine, where it remains true to itself, it is uniquely effective in promoting all that makes man genuinely human.

The elucidation of existence, being directed at no object, leads to no result. A clarification of consciousness stimulates claims but does not bring fulfilment. As cognitive beings, we have to resign ourselves to it. For I am not what I cognise, nor do I cognise what I am. Instead of cognising my existence, I only inaugurate the process of clarification.

Knowledge about man had, on principle, reached its end, when its limitation, in the visualisation of existence, was comprehended. The elucidation of existence, which goes beyond the bounds of this knowledge, must remain unsatisfactory. Upon the basis of the elucidation of existence we move into a new dimension when we attempt a metaphysic. The creation of the metaphysically objective world, or the manifestness of the origin of being, is null if it be divorced from existence. Psychologically regarded, it is only engendered, consists of the forms of fantasy and of peculiarly moving thoughts of the contents of narration and of the construction of being, which vanish into thin air in face of any attempt at comprehensive knowledge. In it man wins repose, or the clarification of his unrest and his danger, when the genuinely real seems to reveal itself to him.

To-day the prolegomena to metaphysics are, existentially, as confused as is all philosophy. Their possibilities, however, have perhaps become purer even though narrower. Because the cogent knowledge of experience was unmistakable, metaphysics is no longer possible after the manner of scientific thought, but must be grasped along an entirely different trend. It has, therefore, become more dangerous than before; for it readily leads, either to superstition accompanied by the repudiation of science and sincerity; or else to the perplexity of those who can make no headway because, although they want to know, they find themselves unable to know. Not until these perils have been seen and endured from the standpoint of existence-philosophy, does the idea of freedom in the grasping of a metaphysical value become possible. What the millenniums have disclosed to man of Transcendence could once again become articulate after it had been assimilated in a changed form.

Ernst Cassirer (1874–1945)

A Clue to the Nature of Man: The Symbol

Best known for his monumental three-volume *Philosophy of Symbolic Forms*, Ernst Cassirer was one of those encyclopedic minds which are rare in any climate but seem to have flourished best in the intellectual atmosphere of the traditional German university. At the age of thirty, he had completed the first two volumes of a history of epistemology, *The Problem of Knowing*, of which the fourth volume was in processs of translation at the time of his death. In 1910 he published his first original work of systematic philosophy, *Substance and Function*. In later years he authored significant studies in such different fields as political theory (*The Myth of the State*), intellectual history (*The Philosophy of the Enlightenment*), philosophy of science (*Determinism and Indeterminism in Modern Physics*), and others. A leading exponent of the neo-Kantian school of philosophy associated with Marburg University, Cassirer left Germany in the year of Hitler's accession to power (1933), moving first to Oxford and later to Yale University.

An Essay on Man, from which the essay that follows has been excerpted, represented Cassirer's effort to compose a brief and relatively untechnical exposition of his theory of symbolic forms. Subtitled "An Introduction to a Philosophy of Human Culture," the book sought to delineate the relevance of Cassirer's paramount "clue" to the nature and culture of man—that is, the *symbol*—in such fields as myth and religion, language, art, history, and science. His essential thesis may be summed up in his statement concerning the contribution of Socrates: "We may epitomize the thought of Socrates by saying that man is defined by him as that being who, when asked a rational question, can give a rational answer. Both his knowledge and his morality are comprehended in this circle. It is by this fundamental faculty, by this faculty of giving a response to himself and others, that man becomes a 'responsible' being, a moral subject."*

THE BIOLOGIST JOHANNES VON UEXKÜLL has written a book in which he undertakes a critical revision of the principles of biology. Biology, according to Uexküll, is a natural science which has to be developed by the usual empirical methods— the methods of observation and experimentation. Biological thought, on the other hand, does not belong to the same type as physical or chemical thought. Uexküll is a resolute champion of vitalism; he is a defender of the principle of the autonomy of life. Life is an ultimate and self-dependent reality. It cannot be described or explained in terms of physics or chemistry. From this point of view Uexküll evolves a new general scheme of biological research. As a philosopher he is an idealist or phenomenalist. But his phenomenalism is not based upon metaphysical or epistemological considerations; it is founded rather on empirical principles. As he points out, it would be a very naïve sort of dogmatism to assume that there exists an absolute reality of things which is the same for all living beings. Reality is not a unique and homogeneous thing; it is immensely diversified, having as

---

*Ernst Cassirer, *An Essay on Man* (Garden City: Doubleday Anchor, 1953), p. 21.

many different schemes and patterns as there are different organisms. Every organism is, so to speak, a monadic being. It has a world of its own because it has an experience of its own. The phenomena that we find in the life of a certain biological species are not transferable to any other species. The experiences—and therefore the realities—of two different organisms are incommensurable with one another. In the world of a fly, says Uexküll, we find only "fly things"; in the world of a sea urchin we find only "sea urchin things."

From this general presupposition Uexküll develops a very ingenious and original scheme of the biological world. Wishing to avoid all psychological interpretations, he follows an entirely objective or behavioristic method. The only clue to animal life, he maintains, is given us in the facts of comparative anatomy. If we know the anatomical structure of an animal species, we possess all the necessary data for reconstructing its special mode of experience. A careful study of the structure of the animal body, of the number, the quality, and the distribution of the various sense organs, and the conditions of the nervous system, gives us a perfect image of the inner and outer world of the organism. Uexküll began his investigations with a study of the lowest organisms; he extended them gradually to all the forms of organic life. In a certain sense he refuses to speak of lower or higher forms of life. Life is perfect everywhere; it is the same in the smallest as in the largest circle. Every organism, even the lowest, is not only in a vague sense adapted to *(angepasst)* but entirely fitted into *(eingepasst)* its environment. According to its anatomical structure it possesses a certain *Merknetz* and a certain *Wirknetz*—a receptor system and an effector system. Without the cooperation and equilibrium of these two systems the organism could not survive. The receptor system by which a biological species receives outward stimuli and the effector system by which it reacts to them are in all cases closely interwoven. They are links in one and the same chain which is described by Uexküll as the *functional circle* (*Funktionskreis*) of the animal.

I cannot enter here upon a discussion of Uexküll's biological principles. I have merely referred to his concepts and terminology in order to pose a general question. Is it possible to make use of the scheme proposed by Uexküll for a description and characterization of the *human world*? Obviously this world forms no exception to those biological rules which govern the life of all the other organisms. Yet in the human world we find a new characteristic which appears to be the distinctive mark of human life. The functional circle of man is not only quantitatively enlarged; it has also undergone a qualitative change. Man has, as it were, discovered a new method of adapting himself to his environment. Between the receptor system and the effector system, which are to be found in all animal species, we find in man a third link which we may describe as the *symbolic system*. This new acquisition transforms the whole of human life. As compared with the other animals man lives not merely in a broader reality; he lives, so to speak, in a new *dimension* of reality. There is an unmistakable difference between organic reactions and human responses. In the first case a direct and immediate answer is given to an outward stimulus; in the second case the answer is delayed. It is interrupted and retarded by a slow and complicated process of thought. At first sight such a delay may appear to be a very questionable gain. Many philosophers have warned man against this pretended progress. "L'homme qui médite," says Rousseau, "est un animal dépravé": it is not an improvement but a deterioration of human nature to exceed the boundaries of organic life.

Yet there is no remedy against this reversal of the natural order. Man cannot escape from his own achievement. He cannot but adopt the conditions of his own life. No longer in a merely physical universe, man lives in a symbolic universe. Language, myth, art, and religion are parts of this universe. They are the varied threads which weave the symbolic net, the tangled web of human experience. All human progress in thought and experience refines upon and strengthens this net. No longer can man confront reality immediately; he cannot see it as it were, face to face. Physical reality seems to recede in proportion as man's symbolic activity advances. Instead of dealing with the things themselves man is in a sense constantly conversing with himself. He has so enveloped himself in linguistic forms, in artistic images, in mythical symbols or religious rites that he cannot see or know anything except by the interposition of this artificial medium. His situation is the same in the theoretical as in the practical sphere. Even here man does not live in a world of hard facts, or according to his immediate needs and desires. He lives rather in the midst of imaginary emotions, in hopes and fears, in illusions and disillusions, in his fantasies and dreams. "What disturbs and alarms man," said Epictetus, "are not the things, but his opinions and fancies about the things."

From the point of view at which we have just arrived we may correct and enlarge the classical definition of man. In spite of all the efforts of modern irrationalism this definition of man as an *animal rationale* has not lost its force. Rationality is indeed an inherent feature of all human activities. Mythology itself is not simply a crude mass of superstitions or gross delusions It is not merely chaotic, for it possesses a systematic or conceptual form. But, on the other hand, it would be impossible to characterize the structure of myth as rational. Language has often been identified with reason, or with the very source of reason. But it is easy to see that this definition fails to cover the whole field. It is a *pars pro toto*; it offers us a part for the whole. For side by side with conceptual language there is an emotional language; side by side with logical or scientific language there is a language of poetic imagination. Primarily language does not express thoughts or ideas, but feelings and affections. And even a religion "within the limits of pure reason" as conceived and worked out by Kant is no more than a mere abstraction. It conveys only the ideal shape, only the shadow, of what a genuine and concrete religious life is. The great thinkers who have defined man as an *animal rationale* were not empiricists, nor did they ever intend to give an empirical account of human nature. By this definition they were expressing rather a fundamental moral imperative. Reason is a very inadequate term with which to comprehend the forms of man's cultural life in all their richness and variety. But all these forms are symbolic forms. Hence, instead of defining man as an *animal rationale*, we should define him as an *animal symbolicum*. By so doing we can designate his specific difference, and we can understand the new way open to man—the way to civilization.

Paul Tillich (1886–1965)

The Courage To Be

Described as "the most enlightening and therapeutic theologian of our time," Paul Tillich incorporated the concerns of existentialist philosophy, neo-orthodox Protestant theology, and psychotherapy within a coherent system of thought. Elaborated in detail in his *Systematic Theology*, that conceptual framework found its most popular and widely influential expression in *The Courage To Be*, published in 1952. In Tillich's view courage is self-affirmation, daring to be oneself: "The courage to be is the ethical act in which man affirms his own being in spite of those elements of his existence which conflict with his essential self-affirmation."* It is significant that this existential concept does not lead Tillich in the direction of that lonely individuality prized by Kierkegaard and Sartre alike (if on different grounds) — rather it leads to the goal of participation and affiliation with others. In this theory of self-realization through genuine communication and reciprocal acceptance, Tillich is at one with other so-called "religious existentialists" such as Buber, Marcel, and Jaspers, as well as with post-Freudian psychotherapists such as Fromm, Sullivan, Rogers, May, and the various schools of *Daseinsanalyse*. Indeed, Tillich has maintained that there exists a close connection between philosophy and clinical psychology, and more exactly that

---

*Paul Tillich, *The Courage To Be* (New Haven: Yale Paperbound Edition, 1959), p. 3.

273

"psychoanalysis belongs fundamentally to the whole existentialist movement of the twentieth century."* The common root and intention shared by both is described as
"the protest against the increasing power of the philosophy
of consciousness in modern industrial society"—the consciousness of Descartes and of the rational-empiricist tradition with its tendency to treat all phenomena, man included,
as specifiable objects of knowledge. "The basic point," he
writes, "is that both existentialism and depth psychology
are interested in the description of man's existential predicament—in time and space, in finitude and estrangement
—in contrast to man's essential nature. . . ." And in his own
writing (as the accompanying selection from *The Courage
To Be* illustrates), Tillich has consistently attended to the
types of existential anxiety which threaten modern man
and which require a therapeutic psychology and theology
for their explication. These anxieties are seen to be not
pathological, not the products of individual neurosis, but
ontological conditions of existence which cannot be "cured"
but only met and coped with affirmatively—through the
courage to be. The function of psychoanalysis and psychotherapy in this regard is that of accepting the patient and
thereby confirming his acceptability, both by himself and
by the world. "In the communion of healing, for example
the psychoanalytical situation, the patient participates in
the healing power of the helper by whom he is accepted
although he feels unacceptable."†

NONBEING THREATENS MAN AS a whole, and therefore threatens his spiritual as well as his ontic self-affirmation. Spiritual
self-affirmation occurs in every moment in which man lives
creatively in the various spheres of meaning. Creative, in this

---

*Paul Tillich, *Theology of Culture* (New York: Oxford University Press,
1964), p. 113.
†*The Courage To Be*, p. 165.

context, has the sense not of original creativity as performed by the genius but of living spontaneously, in action and reaction, with the contents of one's cultural life. In order to be spiritually creative one need not be what is called a creative artist or scientist or statesman, but one must be able to participate meaningfully in their original creations. Such a participation is creative insofar as it changes that in which one participates, even if in very small ways. The creative transformation of a language by the interdependence of the creative poet or writer and the many who are influenced by him directly or indirectly and react spontaneously to him is an outstanding example. Everyone who lives creatively in meanings affirms himself as a participant in these meanings. He affirms himself as receiving and transforming reality creatively. He loves himself as participating in the spiritual life and as loving its contents. He loves them because they are his own fulfillment and because they are actualized through him. The scientist loves both the truth he discovers and himself insofar as he discovers it. He is held by the content of his discovery. This is what one can call "spiritual self-affirmation." And if he has not discovered but only participates in the discovery, it is equally spiritual self-affirmation.

Such an experience presupposes that the spiritual life is taken seriously, that it is a matter of ultimate concern. And this again presupposes that in it and through it ultimate reality becomes manifest. A spiritual self-affirmation: emptiness and meaninglessness.

We use the term meaninglessness for the absolute threat of nonbeing to spiritual self-affirmation, and the term emptiness for the relative threat to it. They are no more identical than are the threat of death and fate. But in the background of emptiness lies meaninglessness as death lies in the background of the vicissitudes of fate.

The anxiety of meaninglessness is anxiety about the loss of an ultimate concern, of a meaning which gives meaning to all meanings. This anxiety is aroused by the loss of a spiritual center, of an answer, however symbolic and indirect to the question of the meaning of existence.

The anxiety of emptiness is aroused by the threat of non being to the special contents of the spiritual life. A belief breaks down through external events or inner processes: one is cut off from creative participation in a sphere of culture one feels frustrated about something which one had pas sionately affirmed, one is driven from devotion to one object to devotion to another and again on to another, because the meaning of each of them vanishes and the creative eros is transformed into indifference or aversion. Everything is tried and nothing satisfies. The contents of the tradition, however praised, however loved once, lose their power to give content *today*. And present culture is even less able to provide the content. Anxiously one turns away from all concrete con tents and looks for an ultimate meaning, only to discover that it was precisely the loss of a spiritual center which took away the meaning from the special contents of the spiritual life But a spiritual center cannot be produced intentionally, and the attempt to produce it only produces deeper anxiety. The anxiety of emptiness drives us to the abyss of meaninglessness

Emptiness and loss of meaning are expressions of the threat of nonbeing to the spiritual life. This threat is implied in man's finitude and actualized by man's estrangement. It can be described in terms of doubt, its creative and its destructive function in man's spiritual life. Man is able to ask because he is separated *from*, while participating *in*, what he is asking about. In every question an element of doubt, the awareness of not having, is implied. In systematic questioning systematic doubt is effective; e.g. of the Cartesian type. This element of doubt is a condition of all spiritual life. The threat to spiritual life is not doubt as an element but the total doubt. If the awareness of not having has swallowed the awareness of having, doubt has ceased to be methodological asking and has become existential despair. On the way to this situation the spiritual life tries to maintain itself as long as possible by clinging to affirmations which are not yet undercut, be they traditions, autonomous convictions, or emotional preferences. And if it is impossible to remove the doubt, one courageously accepts it without surrendering one's convictions. One takes the risk of going astray and the anxiety of this risk upon oneself. In this way one avoids the extreme situation—till it becomes unavoidable and the despair of truth becomes complete.

Then man tries another way out: Doubt is based on man's separation from the whole of reality, on his lack of universal participation, on the isolation of his individual self. So he tries to break out of this situation, to identify himself with something transindividual, to surrender his separation and self-relatedness. He flees from his freedom of asking and answering for himself to a situation in which no further questions can be asked and the answers to previous questions are imposed on him authoritatively. In order to avoid the risk of asking and doubting he surrenders the right to ask and to doubt. He surrenders himself in order to save his spiritual life. He "escapes from his freedom" (Fromm) in order to escape the anxiety of meaninglessness. Now he is no longer lonely, not in existential doubt, not in despair. He "participates" and affirms by participation the contents of his spiritual life. Meaning is saved, but the self is sacrificed. And since the conquest of doubt was a matter of sacrifice, the sacrifice of the freedom of the self, it leaves a mark on the regained certitude: a fanatical self-assertiveness. Fanaticism

is the correlate to spiritual self-surrender: it shows the anxiet
which it was supposed to conquer, by attacking with di
proportionate violence those who disagree and who demon
strate by their disagreement elements in the spiritual lif
of the fanatic which he must suppress in himself. Becaus
he must suppress them in himself he must suppress them i
others. His anxiety forces him to persecute dissenters. Th
weakness of the fanatic is that those whom he fights have
secret hold upon him; and to this weakness he and his grou
finally succumb.

It is not always personal doubt that undermines an
empties a system of ideas and values. It can be the fact tha
they are no longer understood in their original power o
expressing the human situation and of answering existentia
human questions. (This is largely the case with the doctrina
symbols of Christianity.) Or they lose their meaning becaus
the actual conditions of the present period are so differen
from those in which the spiritual contents were created tha
new creations are needed. (This was largely the case witl
artistic expression before the industrial revolution.) In sucl
circumstances a slow process of waste of the spiritual cor
tents occurs, unnoticeable in the beginning, realized witl
a shock as it progresses, producing the anxiety of meaning
lessness at its end.

Ontic and spiritual self-affirmation must be distinguishec
but they cannot be separated. Man's being includes his rela
tion to meanings. He is human only by understanding an
shaping reality, both his world and himself, according t
meanings and values. His being is spiritual even in the mos
primitive expressions of the most primitive human being
In the "first" meaningful sentence all the richness of man'
spiritual life is potentially present. Therefore the threat t
his spiritual being is a threat to his whole being. The mos

evealing expression of this fact is the desire to throw away
ne's ontic existence rather than stand the despair of empti-
ess and meaninglessness. The death instinct is not an ontic
ut a spiritual phenomenon. Freud identified this reaction
o the meaninglessness of the never-ceasing and never-satisfied
ibido with man's essential nature. But it is only an expres-
ion of his existential self-estrangement and of the disinte-
ration of his spiritual life into meaninglessness. If, on the
ther hand, the ontic self-affirmation is weakened by non-
eing, spiritual indifference and emptiness can be the con-
equence, producing a circle of ontic and spiritual negativity.
Nonbeing threatens from both sides, the ontic and the spir-
tual; if it threatens the one side it also threatens the other.

Index

283